Engineer Your Way to Success

America's top engineers
share their personal advice
on what they look for
in hiring and promoting

Published by the

**National Society of
Professional Engineers**®

Text by Shawn P. McCarthy

Proceeds from the sale of this book will go to support programs in engineering registration, engineering ethics, education, guidance, management, legislation, and other areas of benefit to the engineering profession.

For information on becoming a member of the National Society of Professional Engineers, contact the society at 703/684-2810 or visit the society web site at www.nspe.org.

ISBN 0-915409-17-8

NSPE Publication No. 2011-A

Second Edition

National Society of Professional Engineers
1420 King Street., Alexandria, VA 22314

Table of Contents

Acknowledgements

NSPE acknowledges the Professional Engineers in Government (PEG) and the Professional Engineers in Education (PEE) Sustaining University Program (SUP) for their contributions to the second edition of this book. Also recognized for his dedication and commitment to this project is Larry W. Emig, PE.

NSPE appreciates the engineers who gave generously of their time and accumulated wisdom in creating the original book.

Jane C. Ammonds, PE	M.C. Lunsford, PE
Robert Angeli, PE	H. Lee Martin, PE
Louis A. Bacon, PE	Charles McGinnis, PE
James Beavers, PE	Patrick J. Natale, PE
W. Frank Blount, PE	Kermit L. Prime Jr., PE
Harold A. Dombeck, PE	Richard J. Redpath, PE
Fred S. Faber Jr., PE	Francis E. Reese, PE
Gary Garlow, PE	Charles H. Samson, PE
Deborah Grubbe, PE	Gary W. Sproles, PE
E.R. Heiberg III, PE	Carlos C. Villarreal, PE
Joseph R: Keating, PE	Paula Wells, PE
Carroll N. LeTellier, PE	

EngineerYour
Way To Success

Introduction

Let's play a little game.

If you could choose a dozen or so people to have dinner with — any 12 people in the whole world — whom would you choose?

With a little thought, hundreds of names probably come to mind. Maybe you'd pick the President of the United States as choice number one. After that, who knows? Maybe a news anchorman? Maybe a favorite movie star or musician? Maybe a sports figure or two?

But exciting as it would be for you to meet these people, what would it really do for you? As a young engineer, you don't really have an urgent use for acquaintances in the film business or sports. What you really need is a contact or two in the upper levels of the engineering field who will tell you what it takes to make it in their business today.

So let's change the game. Let's say you could invite a dozen, or two dozen, or a hundred presidents, vice presidents, CEOs, and highly placed technical people in the engineering field to your little gathering. Whom would you choose? Now that question's a little tougher. You probably don't even know the names of the people you would most like to speak to.

Well, allow us to give you a little help. Unfortunately, we can't invite you and a hundred industrialists over for sushi and white wine, but we can collect the wit and wisdom of dozens of upper-level engineering executives to share with you. Just sit back and absorb the erudition of a thousand collective years of expertise. Read on, and hear the voices of experience explain what it takes to get ahead in the engineering profession today.

1 Listen Up, Engineers!

This is Experience Talking!

This book is a compilation of input from hundreds of top-level engineers across the country who helped us identify the key factors of success in an engineering career. There is a wealth of material here from a group of men and women who started out much like you — on the first rung of a very tall ladder.

One of the first questions we have to answer is, why do so many engineers — the very men and women who make a living by masterminding the physical details of a project — have such a haphazard approach to the details that make up their own professional career? Developing a career to its fullest potential may be the greatest project an engineer will ever undertake. So why do so many engineers leave so much of their future to chance?

Maybe it's because career success isn't something you can take a course in at school. Career planning is something you're forced into, and you tend to have very short-sighted goals at first. Like a bird that is pushed out of its nest for the first time, your immediate goal isn't to fly south for the winter. Your first order of business is to hit the ground without hurting yourself. Once you learn how to fly, then you start to worry about where your wings can take you.

Identifying the key factors of success is very important to your long-term planning. But first you need to ask, what exactly is a successful career anyway?

Now there's a loaded question. Defining success is like trying to locate the limits of the universe. It's endless and impossible. But within each person there is an individual, finite definition of success that can be realized.

Success may be an abstract concept, but it's fair to make a generalization or two about the word "success" as it applies to a young professional. As a young engineer, you should realize that there are at least three distinct contexts for the term: 1) "Organizational" — in which success means rising to the top. (Note: There are two paths you can follow here, the technical and the managerial. We will talk at length later in the chapter about this fork in the road.) 2) "Professional" — in which the engineering profession has certain values that prescribe what success is, such as service to the public. These are standards that people within the profession hold up as worthwhile and valuable for themselves and their colleagues. 3) " Self-Value" — which is a personal system that is based on your own sense of morality. You alone decide the definitions of success or failure as they apply to your life.

You can establish separate yardsticks of achievement and use them to measure your different contexts of success. But keep in mind that you will probably weigh one of these yardsticks much more heavily than the others. As time goes on, you may also realize that one context of success is more important to you than the others.

As an ambitious young engineer, you may initially feel the tug of all three success contexts at the same time. You are probably looking to earn good money, to attain peer recognition for your professional skills, and to achieve certain personal goals. In time, you may actually do much of what you have dreamed of

doing. But it is also a pretty safe bet that what you define as success today will change several times over the course of your career.

"It seems to me that you can relate success not only to the value system of the individual, but to the individual at different stages of his or her career," a former university president told us. "The value system of the guy or gal just out of school will be different from that of someone who is five years into a career, and completely different from that of the person who is 30 years into a career. Technical knowledge and accomplishments are most important during the first few years. Management and business skills are more important later on. Then, finally, there is appreciation for the arts and an increased sense of the community."

So what should the graduating engineer be looking at? Even if you're looking for money, our sources tell us that if you go after the most lucrative job the first time around, you're overlooking some other significant factors that may maximize your potential in the long run. Money isn't everything. Gaining valuable on-the-job experience is also a big consideration.

"When you're choosing a company, do it the same as if you were choosing a spouse," one industry vice president told us. "If you have to ask if you are in love, you probably aren't. Interview carefully. If someone tells you, 'This is a $7 billion corporation,' your first question shouldn't be, 'How much of that am I going to get?' That kind of question doesn't really have anything to do with your career. The key to getting the perfect job is to say, 'What will I do when I get to your company? Can I see where I will work? Can I talk to someone who does the same job?' These simple questions will reveal a lot to you, and you won't be buffaloed by a lot of sales talk."

"Besides," the vice president of a large architectural engineering firm added, "using dollars as a way of measuring career movement may be convenient, but that's all it is, really. Once you hit a certain point, dollars aren't as important. Other considerations become more important."

Another vice president agreed. "You reach that level of satisfaction, and then you look around you and you say, 'OK, I've been successful, I've been able to achieve certain things.' Then added on to that, you want personal goals. For some people, it's being the best darn engineer at doing a particular function, while others of us want positions of leadership before we consider ourselves successful."

There seemed to be unanimous agreement on this point. Earned money is a great perk. But taken alone, it can't buy success.

Thus, the ultimate definition of success will vary from person to person. But most of the top-level engineers we talked to agree that the factors that lead to strictly professional success do not vary nearly as much. That's why we wanted to isolate and study these factors, to determine how best to relay them to young, upwardly mobile engineers.

The National Society of Professional Engineers surveyed several dozen top engineers around the country, asking them to identify the key factors that determine success in the engineering profession. Most of the engineers we talked to are presidents or vice presidents of large engineering companies. Some are retired admirals or generals. Virtually all of our contacts have achieved a high level of success in their professional career, and they have learned quite a bit about the nature of the engineering profession along the way. Perhaps most important, they scored well in the three measures we mentioned early in this chapter. They all rose to the top of their organization; they gained a great deal of respect from their professional colleagues; and they exhibited a certain self-satisfaction with their life.

Based on the information we received from these experienced engineers, we deduced nine key factors that determine success. These factors are:

1) Technical Skills
2) Judgment

3) Communication Skills
4) Leadership Qualities
5) Management Ability
6) Teamwork
7) Integrity
8) Service
9) Ambition/Hard Work/Commitment

If we had decided to arrange these factors in order of importance, we might have listed integrity right at the top. Almost everyone we talked to said integrity was a major component of success, followed closely by ambition/hard work/commitment. But instead, we decided to list the factors in order of clarity, with those most easily defined taking the top spots. After all, it's easy to determine what technical skills are in the engineering profession. It's much more difficult to define exactly what integrity or commitment are.

Each of the nine factors will be explored in detail in the following chapters. We will begin each chapter with one or two definitions of a given factor, followed by an in-depth look at that factor. At the end of each chapter, we will offer a list of "measures" that you can use to study your own participation and progress for a given factor. These measures are usually offered in the form of a question such as, "Do you sometimes fall asleep and snore during staff meetings?" There are no right or wrong answers to these questions. The measures are simply intended to stimulate your thinking about certain career-related issues.

Additionally, keep in mind that some of our contacts felt every engineer has one very important career choice to make about five or so years after he or she graduates from college. "You will hit a crossroads at that time where you will have to make a decision," a vice president of a construction engineering firm insisted. "Will you concentrate on the technical side, or will you concentrate on management? It's hard to back up once you've picked your path. If, once you start down one road, you decide that you should have chosen the other, you may have to back up, financially or otherwise, in order to switch. In my experience, there is a brief time of a few years when you can go either way. After that, your choice is made. I've seen people with 20 years of technical experience who are great engineers, but they've never established those management skills."

As a young engineer, which path will you choose? Will you be a technical guru? Or will you be a top manager? Is it possible to do both? Read on, and prepare to make your decision.

"Some people think the technical guy will plateau sooner in his career," a company president told us. Others argue that it's false to say that technical is not as good a career path as management. "After all, isn't there usually a technical guru at every company whom everyone goes to when they have a seemingly unsolvable problem? These tech people are highly valued and highly paid. They are successful! True success can be achieved in places other than on the management track."

A good example of this is an earthquake specialist for a major defense contractor whom we talked to. He is considered an expert in his field. He left a management position, where he supervised more than 80 people, to take this specialty position where he could work on his own. He is highly respected, gives talks all over the country, and publishes papers in several engineering journals. He is very highly paid for what he does. In fact, he has even toyed with the idea of retiring at age 55 (he's now 45) to start his own consulting company.

As an earthquake specialist, he may not actually "manage" anymore, but he is still considered a very successful engineer, and he still manages his technology.

"In my case," he said, "I left management to focus on the technical side of engineering, and to make more money. But I will have to say that, in general, the management track in industry may offer greater opportunities at this time to the average engineer. For some reason, many 'wage and salary' organizations view technical work to be less valuable than management work. Perhaps they have a hard time measuring the value of a technical person to their organization. As managers themselves, they know about management work. They know a level-one manager has 15 people under him and gets paid x amount of dollars. They know a level-two manager has 30 people under him and gets paid x amount more money, etc. But they can't as easily measure how valuable some technical people can be to their company.

"Luckily," he continued, "our organization is a little different. We have 'corporate consultant' positions, which are considered to be equal to certain management positions. For instance, my position is listed at the same level as a division manager."

But even when a company recognizes the value of the technical track, it is still difficult for the so-called technical guru to rise to the top of the heap. "The highest-level technical person can expect to make about $75,000 in this company," the earthquake specialist said, "while the highest management person can expect to make up to $150,000."

So who said life was fair?

If such salary discrepancies are really the norm, then why even try to go down the technical path? Why not set your sights on management from day one, and ignore the technical?

Quite simply because there are other opportunities further down the technical path that may not be apparent at first glance.

"I felt that I expanded my opportunities when I switched," the earthquake specialist said. "I am now in a unique, expert field. I enjoy what I am doing very much." He indicated that his sense of job satisfaction now is much greater than when he was in management. He's also not confined to an office anymore. He gets out. He travels around the world. He meets new people.

He also has a valuable skill that can be marketed outside the company. Since he can retire with a pension at age 55, a marketable skill is a real asset. "My opportunities as a consultant are great," he said. "I've built up a reputation." He can go out and establish a second career for himself as an earthquake consultant at any time. Of course, a manager can switch management jobs at any time, too, but there may not be as great a chance to become your own boss unless you have the technical skills to back up your management ability.

Furthermore, a few management positions in each company require very technically oriented people. The engineer with a little bit of management training and a great deal of technical experience could be a shoo-in for such a position.

Reputation building is an important issue to remember for anyone on the strict technical path. Technically oriented engineers tell us that it's important to establish a reputation outside your company to get ahead-even to get ahead within your own company. You build a national reputation by writing papers for technical and scholarly journals, by presenting your papers at conventions, and by joining committees. Once you have a reputation, there is a certain prestige for your company to have you on-staff.

If you are a consultant, they can also rent you out at a hefty profit, and your reputation carries some weight.

"I don't believe the dual ladder theory exists in most companies," one pessimistic manager said. "I think most people who are managers are good technical people who manage by default. Bad managers are often good tech people who shouldn't be managers.

"Ten years ago, my company had a definite technical ladder. It's not so structured anymore. Now, we have absolute technical people who don't manage anything but themselves."

But we found several companies that officially acknowledge the twin tracks. They assign specific titles to certain positions, and technical people can strive to move up to these positions. But when a company does officially recognize the technical track, it's important that it doesn't treat it like a poor stepchild, with little or no support. If that's the case, it's almost better not to have an official technical track. It's better to just allow each person to follow their own path, and to give them the support they need.

Rewarding technical people with their own career path may keep people from entering the management path for the wrong reasons. "You shouldn't become a manager because your wife needs a fur coat or because you're impressed by the title," the director of engineering at a Fortune 500 company told us. "Too many people are socially driven to become the manager because they think it means they're better than somebody else. You shouldn't choose a career in management for the wrong reasons. You have to enjoy managing, and enjoy making a group of people work efficiently. If you don't, you're never going to be that happy, and you're never going to advance to the level of your potential."

But all of this talk about dual career paths may be a moot point if you end up working for a small company with under 100 or so employees. A woman who manages such a company told us that you have to be a jack-of-all-trades in her firm. You can't be strictly on the management track or strictly the technical person. Engineers who need to be strictly technical/research people, because they are absolutely lousy managers, don't really have a place in her group. She needs people who can do a little engineering, a little drafting, a little managing, a little research, and help the rest of the group put it all together in a team effort. If someone is looking for a straight research position, she says, she tells them to look for a large company where they will have that option.

It's doubly important for a technical person to keep current with progress in his or her field — to know the new applications and the theories, applications, and inventions. You have to know what's going on outside your organization in order to survive. "If I hadn't belonged to a professional organization," the earthquake specialist said, "I never would have learned some of the things that I did — things I needed to keep current in my field. And I never would have met some of the people who eventually helped me get ahead."

One thing almost everyone we talked to agreed on was that you can't travel both paths at the same time. Unless you work for a very small company, you can't be both the top manager and the top technical person. As a beginning professional, there is a period when you may be able to do both. Estimates range from five to 10 years into your career. But after that time, a choice has to be made.

"If you go the tech route, it takes too much of your time away from your management duties," one engineer told us. "I have to travel. I have to give papers and study. Meanwhile, things still have to run smoothly when I'm not in the office. Decisions have to be made, etc. Who's going to do my job if I'm off doing something else?"

Occasionally, people do bounce from one path to the other. The earthquake specialist is a prime example of that. But the person who can freely float from management path to technical path and back again is the exception rather than the rule, unless there is a formal structure for such rotation with the company.

"Our company switches people between the technical track and the management track on purpose," said a division manager at a major American chemical supply company. "We do it to broaden people. You don't know what a person's skills are. You may have a technical person who's a real geek, but you may be able to teach people skills to him and build a fine manager. You may also have a good manager who suddenly develops a burr under his saddle and ends up angering everyone he works with. He may start failing on the management ladder, but still be quite successful if he's switched to a more technical job."

"We usually start everyone in a technical job. We believe that engineers have to learn how to be on the team before they can lead the team."

In reality, many engineers start on one ladder and find themselves drawn to the other. But when they change, they usually change for good. In the aerospace industry, you can see several examples of technical people who became managers after working on several projects. Just check the number of managers who have Ph.D.s and research backgrounds! Likewise, we've seen many disgruntled or bored managers who have decided that hands-on work is more to their liking than delegating authority. If they like their new job after the switch, that's usually where they stay, spending the rest of their days tinkering in the lab, sitting at the computer screen, or visiting a building site.

Making the big shift — switching career paths — is nothing to be ashamed of. It could be the wisest career choice of your life. It could lead to a sense of job satisfaction that you previously thought elusive. But it's ultimately up to you to decide.

As an engineer, there is one additional choice you have to make, but it's a choice you probably make before you even finish college. That choice is whether to consider a career in industry, consulting, construction, government, or perhaps even teaching. Will you join a corporate team and work toward refining a new technology? Or will you join a work-for-hire team and apply existing technology toward solving problems for clients? Perhaps government service in a state highway department or a federal agency would appeal to you. Will you teach others your skills? Will you build projects? There is no single golden path to success here. Each avenue is a noble calling.

"Being a consulting engineer requires a different sort of a profile than being an employee in the engineering division of a large company," a long-distance telephone network vice president said. "An engineer with a consulting firm has to understand generic business principles more than an associate engineer in industry. He has to understand profit and loss responsibilities. He has to understand balance sheets.

"The consultant is also more concerned with the application of technology. The engineer doing pure research for a big company is worried more about breakthrough technology."

Occasionally those big companies have to work to make their entry-level engineers think in broader terms than just researching or repairing. "I have 25,000 technicians working for me who are out maintaining our equipment," the executive explained. "One of the biggest problems facing us at the moment is how to get those people refocused from just fixing hardware and installing software to understanding how that technology is modified to solve the end-user's business problem."

As you work out your own definition of success, pay attention to our nine factors. Use them to help you develop a solid career plan, no matter what your goals. And also remember to keep a sense of professionalism in whatever you do. Several of our engineers agreed that getting professionalism into the minds of the young engineers who are entering the field is one of the most important lessons we can teach today.

If this book helps to do that, it will have achieved its goal.

2 Technical Skills

Definition: The knowledge and experience suitable to the demands of the task.

Chances are, no one expected you to be able to tie your own shoes when you were only 1 week old. All you were expected to do was cry, suck on your fingers, and burp. But by the time you were 5 or 6, shoe-tying was one of your expected skills. Any kid worth his weight in milk and cookies could tie shoes, and if he couldn't, he was left behind while the rest of the group scampered off to gym class.

Mastering certain skills has always been a requirement for advancement. As a kindergartner, you couldn't advance to first grade without knowing your shapes, your colors, your alphabet, and your numbers. Twelve years later, you couldn't advance to college without first earning a high school diploma and achieving a respectable SAT score.

In that same vein, you can't expect to move up the engineering corporate ladder, or even gain a foothold on the first rung, without mastering certain skills of your profession. As an engineer, technical skills are the very foundation upon which your career is built. Moreover, if engineering knowledge is an essential starting point, it is also a lifelong process. Rapid technological change means that your engineering education must constantly be updated.

Using a computer as part of your job, you probably know that updated versions of computer software are issued periodically. As a program is improved, new issues may be labeled version 1.1, 1.2, 1.3, and so on.

Now think of your college education as version 1.0 of your engineering education. Periodic updates are necessary, and it's up to you to do the updating.

Don't expect to get your foot in the front door of a company without that "version 1.0" engineering degree, and don't expect to move ahead without staying abreast of new developments. As your career progresses, you will need to update your knowledge and draw upon your ever-increasing experience. You will need to demonstrate that you can use your knowledge to solve problems.

As one manager put it, "You can't just memorize the equations." She added, "You have to show me that you have a thorough understanding of the concepts."

In all honesty, possession of good technical skills is not a real problem for most of you. Engineering graduates entering the profession today are very well educated technically. In fact, their broad-based knowledge is far superior to that of any preceding generation. Most of today's engineers know a little bit about an awful lot of things.

"The trouble is," laments a former university president, "everything in universities today has become crunched. Students may only spend a semester hour or two on reinforced concrete, which to me is ridiculous. But I know they have to squeeze it all in. Students may have the best technical education today, but it may not be as complete as we would like."

"Squeezing it all in" sounds terrible, doesn't it? It brings to mind images of an overstuffed suitcase that you have to sit on just to get it closed. But trying to squeeze it all in is a university's attempt to give students a solid background in the engineering field. (And if the students do all of the required reading, they should be well on their way.)

Yes, education today is often a broad-brush approach. But it helps students gain a foothold. On the flip side of the coin, it's becoming increasingly common for some schools to push specialization in a certain field. A few schools press students to have a specialty by the time they receive their undergraduate degree. But the graduating student may suffer by concentrating on only one area and ignoring the others.

"I think there is a tendency toward specialization," reported a retired general who now runs an international engineering company, "but I take the opposite approach. I know the schools turn out students who are already specialists. They're doing it more and more. But I think we're lacking in what I call the `general practitioner' of engineering — the person who can do a little of everything, and understand even more."

"That's right," a construction company vice president agreed. "No one works in a vacuum. There's teamwork involved, and you have to know about other aspects of a job in order to interact, so you can accommodate them with what you're doing."

Having a specialty may be, well, special. But experienced engineers say that diversity of experience should be a priority for engineers entering the profession today. Get the broad base of knowledge first, and worry about the specialty later. Going on to graduate school is another way of acquiring an area of specialization.

You've got to have a wide range of knowledge. You get it in school, on the job, and through self-study. You can put your hands on more extensive information from a greater variety of sources than in any previous generation, so take the opportunity to diversify your experience as much as you can in your young years. You will thank yourself for it later in life. There will also be opportunities to learn from co-workers.

Your boss may thank you, too. A vice president of a large architectural engineering firm told us, "My background is in the building science field. I'm looking for an engineer who has experience with stadiums, with hospitals, and with government buildings. That's what I mean by diversification, so I can plug him in wherever I need him."

Not all experts agree. The value of diversification is wide open for debate. Another vice president told us that a lot of companies are looking for the highly specialized people who are the best at what they do. If the firm is designing a rocket, they want the engineer who specialized in rocket skin design. They want the best darn rocket skin person they can get. They don't care about his experience in building a hydroelectric dam. However, they may be very interested in his experience in designing an airplane skin. So a little bit of diversification within a specialized field doesn't hurt.

It may be best to say diversity should be attained within the certain technical skills that a person has — designing rockets, working on pharmaceutical products, designing integrated circuits, etc. If you're an aerospace engineer, it's better to work with three or four different groups of people designing a variety of rocket components, rather than three or four groups working on a building, a dam, a computer, and a car.

If you're a computer chip engineer, it's better to go off on a small tangent and work on a computer monitor design than to go off on a big tangent and work in a tractor factory.

The extent of the diversity you need depends on where you are going with your career. If you have defined a path, find out through mentors, co-workers, and friends in the business what sort of experience you will need. If you have not defined your career path yet, look for the broadest base of experience possible.

Our recent survey of top engineers determined that technical challenge and job diversity should outrank all other factors (such as salary, location, and creativity) in selecting first job assignments after graduation. It was clearly indicated in this survey that all other factors responsible for long-term career satisfaction will fall into line more naturally if those twin foundations of technical challenge and job diversity are established as first priorities.

Of course, when recent grads compare job notes, the guy with the highest salary always seems to win the career race. But things change. If making a lot of money in a hurry were your only purpose in life, you might have found an easier way than studying engineering. But you didn't. You most likely became an engineer because it's something you really wanted to do. Don't let the quest for dollars get in the way of your dream, or let a bottom-line offer be your deciding factor when selecting a job.

Consider this story, told by a former electrical engineer who is now the executive vice president of a major long-distance telephone corporation:

"The best engineering job I ever had in my life," he said, "was right out of college, when I went to work for Exxon (then Esso) at a plant in Louisiana. They made me a refinery engineer in their electrical engineering department. I was absolutely shocked at how much they threw at me immediately, and how full-stream it was. In the first six months, I had major lighting projects, large motor installations, protective relay designs for substations, and a whole host of jobs that I didn't feel totally capable of handling given my education.

"But the training was great, and I got the help I needed. They had it set up so that as project engineer, I was also the project manager. So for each new job I had to go out and find the department head who wanted the job done. I would talk to him so that I was clear that I understood his needs. If he needed a new lighting project, the company would assign a draftsman with me, and we would go out to the site and look at the options as to what they wanted done. We would then put pencil to paper and draft out how we would do the job, both the physical and electrical. We would then bring it to the department head to confirm our intent and discuss the options that we had. Then I'd authorize my assistant to go find the parts we needed, from motors to protective relays to wire lights, and more. We actually did the shopping to find the best components for the job. Then I'd ask an instruction engineer to be assigned to me, and when the material came in, he would go out to the site and build. When he was done, we would go out, cut it over, test it, and turn it over to the department head.

"I found after I left that job that I would never again be involved at so many levels of a project. I learned more on that job than in any other I ever had. It was a very diverse education."

Everyone would do well to look for such diversity. And remember, a serious problem with early specialization in a career is this: As technology advances, certain types of jobs may become obsolete. An overly specialized person may be in trouble, while a person with broad-based experience can easily adapt to changes. Also, as the needs of society change, certain specialists will become more valuable than others. Again, the engineer with a broad base of experience can easily move into a new specialty with a minimum amount of training.

"Somebody has planted the idea in young people's minds that they need to job-hop to get diversity, and that's not true," said one vice president when asked if it was best to switch jobs if you want to broaden your experience. "Often you can find the experience you desire right in your current company. We don't want to encourage job-hopping, but we don't recommend limiting yourself either. Loyalty is important, but so is your future." Several of the engineers we talked to felt that diversity within your current company is best. Don't be afraid to change employers if you feel you need to for career growth, they said, but do look within your own company first. A young engineer should feel comfortable asking management for a lateral move in order to gain a variety of experience.

Perhaps most importantly, you should find the areas you are weakest in, and then go out and get experience in them. Experience is the great equalizer. It increases a person's value to a company. It can take a person with a B average from an obscure college and make her as valuable as a new graduate from a top university. Experience means an engineer had the opportunity to learn the ropes. It makes her more competent.

How do employers measure competence? They look at a

number of things. For a new grad, a key component is grade point average. But what if you worked a full-time job while you went to school, and your grades are only so-so? In that case, work experience counts a bit more heavily. But wrapping hamburgers at McDonalds doesn't count. Things that count are, working as a surveyor on a summer road crew, computer knowledge, or a summer technical intern assignment. Other things an employer looks at are: How many years out of school is the person? Does the person have any professional group activity? And, a question that's very important for a beginning engineer, did the person co-op?

Don't underestimate the value of co-oping. It's a foot in the door to the "real world." Many schools have co-op programs at the graduate level now, so if you missed co-oping as a junior or senior, there's still a chance. One engineer we talked to took the five years necessary to get his undergraduate degree through a co-op program. His work at the Georgia Power Co. inspired him to take special design courses as electives that dealt with the application of engineering in the industrial setting, as opposed to the traditional theoretical engineering courses he may have otherwise opted for. His work also helped him clarify what he wanted to do with his life and inspired him to take some management courses. He felt that co-oping helped him make choices that some engineers are not able to make until deep into their careers. He picked his direction early.

One complaint he had is that schools don't do enough to help their students make the management vs. technical or area of practice choices early enough. The burden to choose falls on the young engineer before he or she has had enough time or experience to make a rational decision.

"If I had to advise anyone, even my own son," a director of engineering at a pharmaceutical company told us, "I'd say, 'Go and be a co-op, even if you don't need the money.' That's because co-ops are one of the best places to polish up your technical skills. That's where you learn the lay of the land. In school, you may have learned calculus and a lot of other things that you may never use again, but co-oping helps educate you to the way the business world really works."

"Co-op people have a good reputation," he continued, "and it's funny, because if I had to give a profile of a co-op engineer, I'd say many aren't your 1300 SAT guys and gals. Quite a few of them are people who averaged lower Bs or even high Cs in school, but they value their job very much. There are too many people out there now who think the world owes them a living when they come out of school. The right attitude just isn't there. The co-op people, on the other hand, value their job. If you don't value the job, how is the job going to value you?

"The best attitude is from the person who says, 'I need this job, and I'm going to work hard.' That may seem trite, but it's real. You have to come to the game ready to give. You have to go to the well ready to put water in as well as take out. I think co-ops help create an atmosphere that produces a better engineer. I wish my own son had done it. He had his tuition paid for him. He didn't have to work his way though college. When he got out, he got a job with a major U.S. corporation. Three weeks later, he told me, 'This place is the pits, Dad.' So I told him, 'Come on, that company's supposed to be a great place to work. Maybe you're the one who's the pits, hum?'"

Whether you choose to co-op or not, in the final analysis, what matters most is that you find your strong points and weak points, and learn how you can use your strong points to your advantage. After all, your real worth to a company is in the area where you are the strongest. You should certainly seek out your weak areas and attempt to strengthen them, but your strong area is where you really shine. Don't be afraid to develop it, for your company's sake as well as your own.

Measures

1. Do you feel comfortable with all of the technical aspects of your job? If not, are you studying the material you need to increase your knowledge? If you do feel comfortable, are you working to expand your technical horizons?

2. Take an annual analysis of the publications you read. Are you reading technical journals and periodicals that will increase your knowledge in the engineering field, or do you spend most of your reading time perusing *nontechnical publications*?

3. Are you involved in technical seminars? Do you attend workshops to keep current in your area of practice? Are you, as an individual or assisting a senior engineer, preparing and presenting technical papers?

4. Are you tackling increasingly tougher assignments, or are you doing the same old thing day in and day out?

5. Are you working for a company where senior engineers provide mentoring to assist you in your learning process? Are you taking advantage of mentoring opportunities?

3 Judgment

Definition: The application of knowledge and experience in determining the optimal solution to a given problem.

Did you ever wish that you knew "back then" what you know now?

Did you ever wish that you could go back, maybe to the first year of college, and do everything over again? If you could go back, chances are there's a thing or two you'd do differently. That's because you have better judgment now than you used to. You have more experience upon which to base your decisions, and your logic process is more advanced.

But good judgment isn't a certificate that's awarded to you. You don't walk across the stage, shake hands with a dignitary, and receive a "master of good judgment" degree.

Judgment in engineering is like a sixth sense. If you don't have that sixth sense, developing it can be tough. But you can acquire it through education, training, experience, and perseverance.

You're not going to improve your judgment without a lot of hard work and dedication. The key to improvement is to pay attention. This is so important that it bears repeating...

PAY ATTENTION! Observe as much as possible. Take note of what you see, and file it away for future reference.

Almost as important as paying attention, is having an honest level of confidence both in yourself and what you know. It's important not to confuse self-confidence with good judgment. Nobody likes someone with a "know-it-all" attitude.

The greenhorn engineer may think she knows it all. The experienced engineer knows that she can never know everything — but is confident about what she does know. She has confidence in that finite knowledge base that she has built and knows how to apply her knowledge. For young engineers, the trick is to know how strong their skills really are, and to know when they are in over their heads. All engineers need to be keenly aware of what they do not know. Errors in judgment can often be traced to conclusions drawn from faulty or incomplete information.

Assume nothing!

You know that you are developing good judgment if you find your gut feelings usually turn out to be correct. When everything falls into place exactly the way you thought it would, you should store the results away in your "correct critical assumptions" file for future reference. But be aware, sometimes gut feelings are made before all the facts are in. Don't be ashamed to change your mind when new facts reveal themselves.

One vice president said it this way, "Judgment is an intuitive process based on knowledge and experience that gets me to within 90 percent of the right answer. If my calculations don't bring me within these parameters, then I know either the calculations are wrong, or I must change some critical assumptions gained through experience."

This is an important point. Even the best engineers aren't

always right. But they are right more often than not because they know their business, and they have a knack for using their knowledge effectively. When presented with a problem, an experienced engineer knows almost immediately the general direction in which she will proceed toward a solution. If the research starts to steer her down a different path, she must stop and question her preconceptions. There could be a problem with the experiment. On those occasions when the figures and other research are double-checked and found to be accurate, and they still conflict with her gut feeling, it's time to adjust some of the basic assumptions she made based on previous experience.

Remember, an engineer with good judgment also knows that she's never too experienced to learn just a little more about her job.

Good judgment is a complex issue. It's something that can be shared, but only to a limited extent. Acquiring judgment is a lengthy process, one that can be made easier with the guidance of a mentor. A mentor can't transfer his judgment to you through osmosis, but a good working relationship with a more experienced engineer can go a long way toward helping you achieve your potential.

As the executive director of an engineering membership organization put it, "Judgment is partly intuitive, partly inherited, partly the makeup of the individual, and partly the product of experience and training." Maybe that's why good judgment is so hard to find. You can teach certain aspects of good judgment, but you can't really teach or learn "the whole." The trick is to improve your judgment by consciously paying attention and observing. Try to place the things that you see happening within the context of your job. In other words, try to learn the correct lessons from your experiences.

"Of all of the factors," the president of a large international corporation told us, "judgment is the hardest to fix if there is a problem. I can teach him technical skills; I can teach him to believe in community service. But the one thing I can't teach that cat is good judgment. If he continually confronts me with examples of bad judgment, I may just fire him. I'd fire him because he's dangerous, and I don't know how to change him."

Firing someone for bad judgment? It happens. Good judgment is serious stuff to an engineering firm. This isn't poetry writing they're talking about here. Engineers deal in the physical world, and what they design affects real people.

It's actually good to be a little leery about your judgment and a little nervous at first about your new job. It shows that you have enough sense to know when you're getting in over your head. A construction engineer told us, "I knew my judgment was improving when I finally grew more comfortable with the projects I was working on. I grew more comfortable with the enormous responsibility I had for designing structures that people would be living and working in."

He didn't achieve self-confidence until he was sure that he had the background he needed to produce good judgment. At a certain point, he started making all the right decisions. That's the way good judgment is. You can't always rush it. Like fine wine, judgment sense may have to age a bit before it reaches maturity.

The question is, how do you accelerate the judgment process, given that you have limited experience and are just coming out of college? A key is diversity. With a broad base of experience, you can look at a problem in a number of different ways and find the most logical solution. As the electrical engineer working for Exxon mentioned in the last chapter, a first job with a wide variety of duties is one of the greatest diversity builders (and, it's to be hoped, judgment builders) you can find. He also stressed co-op work as a great experience and judgment builder. In fact, he said, students who did not co-op as undergraduates should think seriously about co-oping if they go to graduate school.

Another engineering firm president illustrated the point with this story:

"Our firm hired two students right out of Penn State, about a year apart. The first one came in, and he was one of those people who had confidence from day one. He was very technically competent. We gave him a lot of responsibility, and he took off like a rocket. Within two years, he wanted to go off to another firm to gain even more experience. He eventually left. But the student who came in a year behind him was what I call a 'plodder.' He had a fine technical background, but he worked at it and worked at it, plodding along. We gave him responsibility much more slowly than we gave it to the other young man. Then, at about five years, it was like a light went on, and then he became more and more confident about what he was doing. Today he is one of our top engineers. I asked him about this once, and he said, `I just didn't have confidence in what I was doing at first.' When he did develop confidence, it made a world of difference. I also know he felt overshadowed by this peer who was working alongside him. People were measuring him against that other young engineer."

Each person's judgment develops at its own rate. In most cases, people do develop. Judgment is the objective. Experience is how you get there. You develop good judgment as you learn from your experiences.

A president of an architectural engineering firm offered a good example of judgment development: "An awful lot of calculations these days are done on computers," he pointed out. "Some younger guys don't know what the programming is behind those calculations, or where the possible weak points are, so they often accept the answer the computer spits out as gospel truth. It takes a guy with experience to look at a computer's answer and say, 'Whoa! That ain't right! Maybe we need to look at this another way.'"

A president of another company agreed. "It scares me when people just rely on the computer," he said. "You can't do that." He noted that a computer calculation may indicate that you need a certain size part for a machine you are designing. What it doesn't tell you is that that is not a standard size. Good judgment would tell you to alter your design slightly to include a standard size part, rather than spend a lot of money to have a special part custom-made when you really don't need it. Without good judgment, you can let your design back you into a corner.

Other engineering executives have indicated to us that good judgment doesn't mean simply coming up with an answer that works. It's coming up with the solutions that best meet the customer's needs. There are thousands of ways to build a bridge, and for any one location there are probably a couple of dozen good designs that would do the job. But the winning design is the one that addresses all of the far-reaching factors involved such as cost, allotted construction time, traffic, available material, environment, aesthetics, and numerous other considerations. Good judgment of a client's needs is an important part of the planning.

Another construction-related example is of a young engineer who is designing a beam to span an auditorium. He might decide on a six-feet-high beam. It would certainly do the job. The trouble is, a four-feet-high beam would stand up just as well in this particular case, and it would accomplish some of the other objectives such as cost savings, easier construction, etc. Likewise, a two-feet beam may also do the job, but it may limit other factors. Using the six-feet beam or the two-feet beam may show engineering knowledge and a limited amount of sense. But deciding on the four-feet beam shows good judgment.

Having good judgment can make you more valuable to a company as you get older — you can find the right answer to a given problem more quickly. Your brainpower becomes of greater value to the firm.

Many engineers we surveyed used the word "comfort" in their definitions of judgment. They said there were times that they weren't "comfortable" with another engineer's proposed solution, or with a computer's calculation. They had a gut feeling, based on previous experience, that something about the answer wasn't quite right. Still other engineers felt that the word "comfortable" doesn't go far enough to raise a red flag when a problem is detected. "I feel that comfortable is an overused word today," said one engineer. "I think it's because people are afraid to speak their minds or insult someone. Instead of saying they feel something is wrong, they say they're not 'comfortable' with it. A better word is `instinct.' Say that something does not feel right because it goes against your 'instincts'."

Sometimes your judgment can serve you in a surprising way, as one general pointed out. "It was winter, 1954," he told us, "during the 'no fire' agreement along Korea's DMZ. I was an army engineer lieutenant, summoned by this grizzled infantry lieutenant colonel whose unit I supported. The colonel pointed to a map on his wall and told me, 'I have 30 tanks and 40 trucks to get across that bridge by nightfall. Can they safely cross?' I rushed to the site in my jeep and pulled out a manual on bridge reconnaissance. With this book and a ruler, I climbed under the bridge and checked the steel, the roadway, and the abutments, and decided it was a close call for the tanks. In front of the colonel an hour later, I said, 'Sir, the trucks are okay, though I'd send them over one at a time. But the tanks are too much for that bridge by maybe 30 percent. And I could see no ford nearby.'

"The colonel asked if the calculations included a safety factor. I didn't know, and I told him so. I did mention that the manual explained that a bridge crossing could occur 'at risk.' Such a crossing should occur slowly, with no gear changes, with only one vehicle at a time on the bridge. Even then, I told him, I felt the tanks weighed several tons more than the bridge could safely handle.

"The colonel thanked me and dismissed me. It was clear that he intended to use the bridge. I wondered, should I report him to my engineer superiors, and avert a bridge failure and perhaps injuries? I reviewed my calculations again and took into consideration the fact that the bridge was in pretty good shape. I had also seen a lot of traffic on the bridge over the past few months. Several vehicles at a time rolled across it with no problems. I eventually concluded that I would be comfortable with driving a tank over that bridge, very slowly, with no other vehicles on the bridge. I knew that my advice to the colonel had signaled the need for care and caution, and the colonel   appeared to be the type who would pass such advice along and see that it was enforced. I decided not to make the call to my superiors.

"At breakfast the next morning, the engineering company commander asked me if I heard that the 160th Regiment, with a battalion of tanks, had changed sectors. I said I heard that they might change, and added, 'I hope they crossed that bridge gently.'

As a young man, the general used his judgment to reach a conclusion that didn't seem apparent at first glance. Perhaps he followed these four simple steps for good judgment:

1) He knew the quality of the work (research, personal observations) he was dealing with.

2) He was confident about his application of technique.

3) He had a gut feeling that the results were right.

4) He had the ability to admit when his knowledge and experience were inadequate for a given task. (In this case, identifying a margin of error for the colonel.)

Measures

1. Do you make the same mistake more than once?

2. Observe to whom the boss gives the tough assignments. (When a really important job comes along, he or she will almost always give it to the engineers who consistently display good judgment.)

3. From whom do your peers seek advice? At every company, there are usually one or two people who are known to have good judgment. Co-workers often seek these people out. They may ask these people technical, or sometimes even personal, questions. Do your peers ever seek advice from you?

4. Are you suffering from lack of self-confidence? Are you working to improve your knowledge and experience in your weak areas in order to overcome that feeling?

5. Are you making judgments on a consistent basis and within your level of expertise? It is necessary to be making judgment calls, or you are not progressing in your engineering career.

4 Communication Skills

Definition: Ability to analyze the audience and convey information with clarity and effectiveness.

There is no better example of the importance of communication skills to an engineering project than the biblical story of the Tower of Babel.

When the people of the ancient land of Shinar began their project, they intended to build a tower that would reach to heaven. But divine intervention caused mass confusion when everyone on the work site began speaking a different language.

When they couldn't communicate effectively, they couldn't interact as engineers and builders. The Tower of Babel was never completed.

Even today, when satellites and fiber-optic cables beam messages around the globe to millions of people, there is still a great need for simple, effective, one-to-one communication. But too often, young engineers have ignored the chance to develop their communication skills. It's understandable. When there is so much pressure to gain technical knowledge, it's tempting to pass up the university classes that might enhance writing skills or other communication arts to concentrate on math and engineering classes.

As we pointed out in Chapter 2, today's engineering grads are extremely well educated technically. But they may not have the broad base of other types of education that grads 20 to 30 years ago had. Noticeably absent are good communication skills.

"That's a real problem," an industry vice president told us, "because the single greatest factor for advancement today is communication skills. Skilled engineers may be in short supply, but technical competence can always be purchased. However, people who communicate well are extremely hard to find. I think a good communicator is someone who can take a complex issue and explain it in layman's terms. Listening well is equally important; you have to know what the layman needs and wants."

A young engineer told us, "It's important for engineers, at any point in their career, and especially during the first five to 10 years, to make sure that they are not operating in a vacuum. You need constant feedback from your peers, your managers, and your subordinates," she explained. "If you are constantly open to feedback, or `reciprocal influence,' as we call it today, you will be able to know whether or not things are going well, and if they're not, you're going to know why very quickly."

We know of one instance in which a young engineer who was looking for a job wrote directly to the president of a firm. Unfortunately, his letter was full of misspellings, punctuation errors, and other examples of extremely poor writing. The company president was so outraged that he marked up the corrections and mailed the letter to the head of the English department at the university from which the young man was graduating. The English professor eventually forwarded the letter to the engineering professors who had taught the student.

All of that embarrassment could have been saved if the student had taken the time to learn how to write an effective business letter and to double-check his spelling before sending the letter on its way.

"Every person should have a dictionary and the style manual [the manual followed by his particular firm] on his desk," an engineering professor told us. "Use them. The more you use them, the less you will eventually have to use them. It really is devastating when you pick up work from a Ph.D. candidate and find he can't write a grammatical sentence. To me, I just wonder, 'What in the world are you doing?'" Engineers today should also utilize word processing software to efficiently and effectively edit letters and manuals.

"It's unfortunate," an industry vice president lamented, "but these days, most engineers get their education in numbers, rather than words. We need to expand their communication training. I know that course loads are tight, but I believe that if you have just one elective to take, it should be used to take a communication course. That's what's going to earn you the dollars down the road. If you have to go back to school to take such a course, do it. Most local community colleges probably have night courses in improving communication skills that you can sign up for. It's worth the trouble."

Is it even worth taking an extra college semester to beef up communication skills with classes that you couldn't work into your regular schedule? This moves us quickly into the "five-year B.S." area that some students dread. From the hiring company's standpoint, extra classes are a good thing, but from the student's perspective, there has been enormous resistance. Students want to get out of school and get into the job market. They want to stop spending money on higher education and start earning some real money of their own for a change.

At the very least, education in other areas, such as effective writing or public speaking, should be an ongoing process.

Night classes and weekend seminars are available in most cities. Check newspapers and the phone directory. Inexperienced engineers may need to start supplementing their basic education rather quickly if they expect to move up.

Keep in mind that communication skills are especially valuable to consulting engineers who are involved in many public hearings. Civil engineering projects are subject to many local laws and environmental policies. The clients need to know that you know what the laws are and that you will conform to them.

"When you're talking with a client or a potential client," the president of a consulting firm said, "stand on your own two feet and openly discuss your ideas, their ideas, and other people's ideas. Do it with a degree of competence that comes across to them and impresses them that you know what you are talking about. But talk to them on their level."

That means, when you're giving a presentation to laymen, keep the language simple. Don't try to impress people, because you may just end up confusing them or angering them. If you have to use a big technical word, or an obscure engineering term, explain what you are saying in a non-condescending tone, or say, "As you may know, _____means _____" That way, you're hinting that some of them probably know what the term is, but you're explaining it for the others in the group who may not.

Likewise, when you have to make a presentation to a group such as a town council or a city advisory commission, it's not a good idea to pile on technical details until everyone in the place is shuffling their feet and looking out the windows. Know what they need to hear.

Our definition at the beginning of this chapter says that communication skills include the ability to "analyze the audience." This term implies two-way communication. It includes listening and other critical devices used to understand the audience.

These other devices include knowing a bit about the audience that you are talking to. What language do they speak?

Are they engineers? Are they laypersons? Are they politicians? A successful engineer is one who can convert technical language into the language of his or her audience and convey complex information in simple, non-technical terms.

"Be aware of how much information you need to give someone," one of our corporate contacts told us. "They want to know what time it is. They don't want to know how to build a watch." He's right on the mark. Information overload is a common error for engineers. In practical terms, he means that a town council wants to know that their new sewer plant will meet current EPA standards, that it will last x number of years, that it will handle their current sewage needs and allow for the expansion of x number of new buildings in the town. If there are any unknowns in the project, the council will want to know those, too. They probably don't want to know the exact size of all the pipes you will install, or how many cubic yards of cement you will need to pour for the building footings. They might not even want to know what the horsepower of the pumps will be. You probably shouldn't dump all of those specifics on the council members unless they ask for them.

"Be aware," a consultant warns, "there is such a thing as being too good a communicator. I know it sounds strange, but there is a fine line that you can't cross. You have to appear sincere. You can't be so slick with your public relations that you appear plastic. People will think that you are hiding something. Be real. Talk as a friend and an equal when you are talking to clients."

A successful engineer can analyze how much information the audience wants and needs, and provide it accordingly. This is as true when dealing with your boss as it is when dealing with a non-technical client.

As a young engineer, you may not have good communication skills yet. If that's the case, you should not feel concerned, however it is important to improve these skills. "People seem more open to constructive criticism on their technical skills than on their communication skills," the vice president of a firm told us with a note of disgust in his voice. "Don't think someone is nit-picking when they criticize your communication skills. Listen and learn from it!"

Equally important is the ability to organize your thoughts and present them to the boss. When you're new, the boss probably wants to hear your solution and a little bit about the thought process you used to come up with it. After you've proven yourself, he or she probably won't want to hear every minute detail of how you reached your conclusions, or how you formulated your proposed design. As a manager becomes increasingly familiar with how you work, you can let that work speak for itself.

Just as you wouldn't run straight to the boss every time you found a problem, you shouldn't expect the boss (or a secretary) to clean up your sloppy writing or poor presentation. Put some effort into it, even if it takes a little time. In most firms, a good finished product is more important than the time it took to prepare it. (Within reason, of course. No one will let you spend two months on a two-page proposal!)

The flip side of the "know your audience" coin is knowing how much information to share with your co-workers. While a town council may not need to know the specifics of your design, some of the people in your office who are facing a similar design problem may be very interested in your solution to a particular problem. Sharing information can be extremely important in these circumstances.

"When I find out some guy's been sitting on some information that I need," an engineering firm vice president told us, "and I ask him why he didn't give it to me, and he says, 'Well, you didn't ask,' I think, "Boy, maybe I didn't ask you, but you certainly aren't rising to your potential!"

Communicating with, and helping, your co-workers is good for a firm, and it's usually good for the young engineer, too. Sharing information around the office is an important function that makes everyone's life easier. Our chapter on teamwork will go into this in more detail.

All of this leads us to "assumptions." You need to know

what your audience's assumptions are in order to deal effectively with them. Deductive reasoning is based on two
assumptions called the major and the minor premise. A conclusion is drawn from these. Persuasion theory teaches that
you should discover audience assumptions and use them in
developing your conclusions. You do not argue with your
audience's conclusions because they have already reached
their conclusions and believe in them. Instead, you change
audience opinion by changing their assumptions, and letting
new conclusions follow deductively. The successful persuad-
er asks questions first to determine audience assumptions.

Poor communication can destroy even the best laid plans
before they ever get off the ground. Usually it's because the
explanation of an engineer's conclusions fails to satisfy the
questions of the customer. A former general with the U.S.
Army Corps of Engineers gave us this prime example:

"We were looking for a cost-effective way to stem the
killing influx of a hurricane-driven tide into a lake area," he
said. "The most cost-effective way was to construct gates at
the entrance to the gulf. Levees could also protect the popu-
lated areas, but building those would be far more expensive.
Each solution would bring along its own set of environmental damages. So the project was explained to those on the
north side of the lake. They weren't convinced, so their
leaders were flown by government plane to the Waterways
Experiment Station in Mississippi, where a model would
show the conclusions in a way the layman could compre-
hend. Later, at a hearing on this project, a very vocal group
in the audience — mostly from the north side of the lake —
shouted the hearing officer down and ridiculed the presentation. Subsequent press reports and the ensuing state and
congressional reactions were negative. The gates were not
approved. The levees were raised instead."

That's an important lesson to learn. Make sure that the
explanation you provide satisfies the customer's questions. If
it doesn't, you're going to run into trouble down the road.

Some of the managers we talked with felt that good com-

munication has four distinct subcategories. These are:
1) Speaking
2) Writing
3) Graphics (sketching and reading diagrams)
4) Listening
A good engineer needs to develop his or her abilities in each of these areas before being considered a good communicator.

The first two, speaking and writing, seem pretty basic. Either you can speak well, or you can be trained to. Those who are good speakers can usually make their point with a minimal amount of confusion. They can also tailor their talk for the layperson or the technical expert, as needed. The good writer can keep his or her reports concise and to the point, without spelling, grammatical, or punctuation errors.

But let's take a closer look at these skills. Presentations demand good oral skills. You may have to sell a concept, defend a budget, or explain progress (or a lack of it) on a project. All of these require solid oral presentation skills. One vice president said, "I can work a potential client on a multimillion-dollar project for months and know a good deal will ride on the project engineer's oral presentation to the client. Young engineers need to get themselves ready for that moment when the contract award is influenced by their ability to gain immediate respect from the client in an oral presentation."

Another vice president told us that joining Toastmasters, a nationwide public speaking organization with branches in most major cities, was one of the best things he ever did to enhance his public speaking abilities.

Written skills demand a certain expertise, too, and virtually everyone can use some improvement. You should work to become a literary critic of sorts on good engineering papers, reports, and articles. Analyze them to determine how they are structured, organized, and written. Make note of bad examples when you see them. After all, critical reading skills help develop good writing skills.

Graphic skills are a little tougher to put a handle on. Engineering graphics is a type of language unto itself. You learn this language on the job and in school. It's a series of symbols, lines, and other marks that are used to tell a story. Reading the symbols correctly unlocks that story for an engineer.

"You know," the vice president of a large architectural engineering firm joked, "it's often been said that an engineer can't explain anything if he doesn't have a piece of paper and a pencil." His point is well taken. All of the words and hand gestures in the world can't do the work of a simple schematic drawing. A good drawing does wonders toward helping other engineers know what you're thinking. As an engineer, it's part of your language.

Just as you can work to develop your oral and written skills, you can work to enhance your understanding and use of graphic representations. You learn by doing. You read, you experience, and you grow. But some people will always use graphics a little better than others. The best graphics people seem to have an uncanny ability to see things in three dimensions, and then show them in two dimensions. This may be difficult to teach but necessary to do.

Listening may be, the most important communication skill of all. It's crucial to understanding your customer's needs, your boss's expectations, and your colleague's ideas. Make a special effort to learn how to ask effective questions and listen to the answers. You should spend more than half the time in any conversation listening.

In Chapter 1, we mentioned that there comes a point in everyone's career when he or she has to choose between the management path and the purely technical path. Communication skills may play a big part in that choice. The ability to communicate effectively is quite desirable if you venture down the technical path. It is absolutely essential if you are on the management path. We'll take a closer look at this in Chapter 4.

Measures

1. How many questions must a reader ask before the intent of your written work is clearly understood? Also, how often does your boss ask you to rewrite your documents?

2. How many people, and what type of people, can you stand up in front of to speak before you suffer from inhibiting anxiety? In some cases, numbers aren't as important as the type of audience. You may be able to stand up in front of 50 cub scouts but have a hard time speaking before two managers. Work to be able to speak to ever-increasing numbers of people, and work to control your nerves when you meet with important and influential people. Could you make a presentation in front of a city council, which may have up to 10 members, plus a large audience of news reporters, attorneys, and other prominent spectators? Could you make a presentation in front of the Board of Directors of your corporation? Could you make an effective presentation in front of your mirror? (Note: Being nervous isn't always a bad thing. A lot of good work has been done with sweaty palms.)

3. How many papers do you submit to engineering conferences or to publications? (Note: Some employers do not permit their employees to write such pieces on company time, so some people will have more opportunity to publish than others. But it may be an indication of your drive and initiative if you're willing to write professional pieces on your own time.)

4. How frequently do you receive meaningful compliments on your written work or on your oral presentations? How frequently do your readers or listeners seem confused and full of questions? How frequently are you asked back to speak again, or invited to submit a new paper?

5. Are you able to write your reports or prepare your oral presentations within your budgeted time?

5 Leadership Qualities

Definition: *The ability to motivate others to move with enthusiasm toward a goal that is seen with a passion.*

In the military, one of the first things a new recruit hears at boot camp is that he has to learn how to follow before he can even think about leading. Although the recruit may not think so at the time, this is actually very sound advice. The so-called "followers" of the world are the people who ultimately decide who their leader is. Calling someone a leader and giving him rank isn't always enough. If the followers don't believe in their leader, there can be trouble. When the going gets tough, the leader may turn around one day to find there's no one behind him.

Many engineers don't realize it, but leadership ability is very important in their chosen profession. Sometimes you need to get people to come along with you — to see things your way — when you have a breakthrough idea for a project.

We asked a trio of retired Corps of Engineers generals what they thought a good leader was made of. They gave us some good tips, but surprisingly, they said they found it difficult to come up with a single clear-cut definition of good leadership.

"At West Point," one of them said, "we were asked to list what are commonly considered the characteristics of successful military leaders. Most people could come up with eight to 12 good characteristics. But then they could also come up with 10 leaders who were obviously successful folks, you know, the Napoleons and so forth, who didn't fit the mold. Such leaders might have had six or eight of the characteristics, but they were decidedly lacking in the others. Some were even contradictory. In theory, they shouldn't have made good leaders at all! But if we go deep enough, we usually find that the leader knew what his weaknesses were and found some way to compensate for them. Sometimes he compensated by getting a deputy or an assistant who provided that skill that he lacked."

"We can't say that there is a single model for a leader," another general added. "There are too many variables."

The basic answer is they can't fully describe good leadership, but they know it when they see it. "Good leaders are people you can trust," the first general said, "and they are people who create positive regard in others who work around them."

A manager in a large chemical company put it this way: "A true leader takes the risks. A true leader will trust someone when the person may or may not trust back. A true leader will open up that trust, betting on the person to respond in kind. That's what makes leadership qualities something special.

"There are talented people at every level of the organization," she added. "All one needs to do is allow that talent to show and bloom forth. You have to approach every person with the thought that you can learn something from them. I can learn something from everybody I meet. Therefore, every person I meet has a certain worth, no matter what their position, from the janitor to the head of the company.

"Unfortunately, most people just give up on others too easily. They write people off. They never say, `Well, I'm going to try.' That's not what a good leader does. Of course, this type of personal interaction is much easier when done on a one-to-one basis rather than one person to a whole company, but you have to start somewhere. The place to start practicing and building these skills is when you are an entry-level manager or worker."

Sometimes the best leader is the person who didn't set out to be a leader. She's the one who rose to the challenge when it was presented to her. "I think leadership can be learned," an industry vice president said, "but just as with communication, there is a structured part, and a part that is learned through experience. It takes time and effort to cultivate a leadership role. It comes with practice."

One industry manager strongly supported the idea that leadership ability is something you can acquire. "The belief that leadership can't be taught is BS," he said, "and when I say BS, I'm not talking about anything organic. This BS stands for a 'Belief System.' It means something that we have come to believe through whatever system of teaching that we may have — the system responsible for molding and shaping our opinions. One of the things our belief system has taught us is that great leaders aren't trained, they are born. That's a false assumption. That's BS.

"Now this doesn't mean that there aren't leaders who have greater genetic skills that allow them to do some things more effectively. Of course there are some people like that. That's not the point. The point is that all of us can become better in leadership skills by learning and applying techniques that are taught in leadership seminars, etc. You often find such seminars or courses in continuing education programs at local colleges. You can also find a few leadership courses listed under the management classes at these colleges.

"There will probably always be a school of thought that leadership can't be taught, that it's something you're born with. But when people say that, I like to ask them, 'Would you like to be operated on by a surgeon who learned his trade at the local butcher shop? Would you like to hire an engineer who's never been taught anything, but who would like to try to build a bridge anyway?' Of course you wouldn't. 'So how long would you follow a leader who never learned the best way to lead?' I feel that leadership is definitely a skill that can be taught. It needs to be taught, and it's something that young engineers need to learn.

"Saying that leadership can't be taught is just a paradigm that you believe. A 'paradigm,' by the way, is a term adopted by Joel Barker to mean a set of rules and regulations that define boundaries and teach you what to do to be successful within those boundaries.

"In my mind, a paradigm leads to a belief system. If you set boundaries too tight, and you believe that leadership can't be taught, then it can't be. If you believe that leadership can be taught, then you will find ways to teach it."

In fact, one of Joel Barker's favorite sayings is, "I'll see it when I believe it," rather than the old standby, "I'll believe it when I see it." In other words, you can make things happen when you believe that you can make things happen.

The difference between a leader and a manager is like the difference between effectiveness and efficiency.

"Efficiency" means doing things right.

"Effectiveness" means doing the right thing.

The difference between these two words is important. You can do things right, but be working on the wrong things. You can be efficient as heck, but not very effective.

What you are aiming for is to do the right things the right way, and that means you have to have a combination of efficiency and effectiveness. A good manager controls the efficiency aspect. A good leader controls the effectiveness aspect. A truly great manager or leader can combine both skills.

A researcher recently identified a group of corporate Chief Executive Officers (CEOs) who were nationally recognized for building successful organizations while maintaining high employee loyalty. When the researcher interviewed employees of these CEOs to see what characteristics established their boss as a leader in their minds, four common characteristics emerged:

1) A leader is someone who has a vision that is seen with a passion. The leader sees something that can be accomplished and convinces others that doing it is in their collective interest. The vision is accepted by the followers as a worthy goal and becomes a motivating force.

2) The leader listens. The leader discovers the assumptions of the followers and uses them in portraying the value of the goal. The leader is constantly assessing the assumptions of the followers by listening to them.

3) There is trust involved. The leader can be trusted to value the interests of the followers. You obey authority, but you trust the leader.

4) A leader has positive regard for his or her followers. The leader enhances the self-confidence of the follower. (After all, if a leader thinks all of his followers are jerks, how good a leader can he really be if jerks are the only people who will follow him?) People feel better about themselves after working in concert with a good leader. The leader shows how striving for the goal is self-rewarding.

In the most basic terms, a leader is someone whom you choose to follow. You may be required to follow a manager, but he or she may not be the person in the company who *truly* inspires you to do your best.

Looking at the qualities of exceptional people can best outline leadership. For example, Arthur Lang, a psychologist and management consultant at UCLA, says that leaders are exceptional people, and great leaders exhibit the following characteristics:

1) They have pride in who they are and what they can do. They want to make a difference.

2) They do their work with enthusiasm.

3) They believe that they are engaged in meaningful work, and believe that through this they can and will make a contribution.

4) They believe that they give and receive value and recognition for their efforts and for the efforts of other people.
5) They have a greater perceived confidence and competence than the norm. They know their priorities and they follow their priorities. In other words, they have a plan and they work the plan.
6) They have greater perseverance. A winner is the person who always gets up after he or she gets knocked down. They are the ones who say, "I'm going to complete this work, no matter what."
7) They are willing to take mental, verbal, and behavioral risks. This doesn't mean that they are adventurers, but it means they are willing to ask the controversial questions when necessary. They are willing to take the risk, even in situations where such risk-taking might not be the norm.
8) They have listening skills. One of the most important parts of communicating is listening.
9) Leaders can articulate well. They can get their point across effectively and sway opinion.
10) Leaders must be ethical. They must behave ethically in order to instill the trust that is necessary for them to be leaders.

"I have learned that there are five drivers of behavior," an industry manager said. "These five choose you, you don't choose them." The five are:

1. Thinking Styles

"How often have you thought about thinking? How often have you thought about thinking differently? Believe it or not, you can be taught to recognize thinking styles, and you probably have a preference for your own thinking style. While you probably won't change your personal preference, you can learn to reorganize your thoughts. You can recognize thinking styles in others and change your questioning techniques as you approach a problem. This will help you to add new thinking-style tools to your leadership tool kit."

He offered the following examples of "thinking styles": a) the synthesis thinker, b) the idealist, c) the realist, d) the analyst, and e) the pragmatist:

2. Motivation

"How motivated are you to do things differently? How hungry are you for improvement and change?"

3. Sensitivity

"How sensitive are you to the feelings of other people? Are you a high screener or a low screener? In other words, do you screen out emotions, or do you sense what others feel?"

4. Role Playing

"People play different roles in different situations. Does your role as a manager, leader, mother, father, club member, etc. affect the way that you behave?"

5. Reality

"Can you step back and review the reality of a situation when you are close to it? What do you believe are real solutions to your problems?"

Looking at the *five drivers of* behavior listed above, we may assume that the first driver, your Thinking Style, probably chose you by genetic background *or* upbringing, but you can choose to modify that style and improve your thinking.

The other four drivers all influence the way that you think. All of these things can be evaluated and improved, and they can greatly affect your leadership skills.

Measures

1. Are you often selected by your peers as team captain? As group leader? As chapter president? As the head of anything?

2. Analyze your current leadership responsibilities. You should always be performing some leadership function at work, at church, at a community group, or for a professional society.

3. What is your "followership?" Look behind you. Is anyone following?

6 Management Ability

Definition: *Ability to organize resources and coordinate the execution of tasks necessary to reach a goal in a timely and cost-effective manner.*

Is there a person in the working world today who doesn't look at the actions of his or her boss and think, "That's not the way I'd do it?" The fact is, everyone has his or her own opinion on how to manage. Everyone thinks they could do a better job than the next guy. But until you actually sit in the management hot seat, it's hard to realize just how difficult management can be.

After all, there are management skills, just like there are technical skills, communication skills, etc. You have to have the skills in order to do the job. Just as there's no standard way to lead, there's also no standard way to be a manager.

Yet everyone knows a good example of bad management when they see one. Management is a balancing act, and it's a lot easier to fall off the high wire than you might think. A key to successful management is planning, and then updating the plan as things progress. It's keeping a handle on things and leaving as little to chance as possible.

There is no way that we can outline modern management philosophy in one short chapter. If management is a solid career goal for you, it is wise to read up on the subject in other publications. There is a wealth of good reference material on this subject. Almost every week there are new books on the subject of management: how to manage people, how to manage time, how to manage money, how to manage resources, and how to manage managers. You can never read all of the management books. If you bothered to read just a dozen such books, you'd probably find a dozen different management theories.

But that doesn't mean you shouldn't read the books. Read them anyway, even if some of the theories seem contradictory. Understand the different theories, and apply them as needed to your own situation.

In this chapter, we'll talk about the manager as salesman, the manager as team-builder, and the choices you have to make between a management and a strictly technical career. But first, let's talk about what management is.

Management encompasses a lot of things. At its most basic level, it's how well we identify, develop, and utilize resources. A good manager is someone who can do all three to get a job done. A successful manager must also be able to manage people, money, materials, and time.

People management is perhaps the most important of all. If you manage your people properly, the other resources should fall into place. (Note: In the engineering field, material management ranks a very close second to people management.)

Let's take a closer look at resource management to get an idea of what's involved.

Identifying Resources

You need to know what's available to you to get your job done right. You need to know who your people are and what they are capable of doing. If you don't know, ask. Or have someone prepare a report. You need to know what equipment you have, and how it can be applied to your specific needs. You need a budget. You need office supplies. Take a second look at some of the unused equipment in your company. Determine if you can use that equipment to serve your needs. Take a look at old research done on previous projects. Can any of that research be applied to your project?

You need to know what you have to work with before you make plans. That's the only way you can decide where to channel worker energy and how to spend your budget.

Developing Resources

There may be more resources available than are initially obvious. It is important to be creative. Several years ago a manager had to be the first person to determine that a computer used for calculations could also be used to manage the payroll. Find out if there are new technologies that can be applied to your needs. Technology and software are continuously being updated, therefore keep current on new software available. Make sure you have identified all of the experts inside or outside of your company that you can call on for advice. Make sure that you keep abreast of all of the resources available in your particular field by reading trade magazines and other publications.

Utilizing Resources

After you have identified and/or developed resources, you have to apply them to the work at hand. Delegate work and have high expectations for output. Make sure the work flows smoothly from one department to the next. Keep an eye out for bottlenecks. Work on processes that interact with timing, organizing, staffing, coordinating, and budgeting. Be the first to apply a new technology to your company's needs. Do the best with what you have, and always keep an eye out for more.

Now let's take a look at some of the other aspects of management.

People Management

The morale of the people under your charge must be good in order for them to take pride in their jobs and do their work efficiently. The work produced by your people will be a direct result of your ability to guide and coach them. You may be an excellent problem solver, but the trick is to get other people to take on this responsibility. As an effective manager, you shouldn't have to do everything yourself. You should be able to motivate others. After you have prioritized and discussed the assigned tasks and the schedule to complete the work, give employees some rope, but be available for consultation. Remember that making mistakes can be an excellent teacher. A person who has never made a mistake, most likely has not advanced very far in his or her career. Remember, too, that people like praise, even for small accomplishments. If you are a good manager, people will want to work in your department.

"One of my favorite quotes," said one manager, "is 'All people are not created equal, but they should be given an equal opportunity.'"

Money

Bringing a project in over or under budget is an indication of your ability to handle several aspects of your management job. A manager has to sweat both the macro and the micro costs to keep everything in line. You have to worry about the financial condition of your company, the cost of the product, the cost of salaries, and the cost of paper clips. You have to be able to prepare a budget in the first place and justify it to whoever controls the purse strings.

Material

Make sure you have what you need to do your job. If you don't have what you need, make sure you have people working on getting it. Have you estimated carefully? You cannot afford to run out of material before the work is done. Likewise, you can't overestimate and saddle your company with material it doesn't need.

Time
The timeliness with which an assignment is completed reflects your ability as a manager. You must delegate and empower people to do their work within the time allotted. Obviously, if a deadline has to be missed in order to make sure that a product functions safely and is properly tested, then most engineers will trade the deadline for a quality job. The space shuttle Challenger accident is the most compelling example of making the wrong choice to honor a deadline. But be aware that constant delays affect the integrity of a company. For instance, stock values of software engineering companies have been known to fall when the company delays the release of previously announced products. And delays in construction projects often impact a firm's profit margin.

To sum it up in a single word, one industry vice president said, "Managers are involved in *selling*. What they are selling is a service, and service is usually a high-communication area where you need to interact. You meet a lot of people. You draw on their experience. You exchange ideas and use those ideas to draw on your own experience. You can't be shy if you are a manager. If you are, you are not properly representing your department, your subordinates, or your company. You also can't be unorganized. You have to keep track of all of your resources, time, and money, and treat everyone fairly. You must create a sense of purpose and provide the means to achieve it."

Building and Working with Teams
One experienced manager said, "As a manager, you must have an ability to get along with people and to build teams. Successful teams make a successful manager, so you must build your team carefully. But the biggest thing is to share

credit. Don't take all the credit for yourself. People will work extra hard if they know they will share in the praise for a job well done." You will be surprised what can be accomplished if no particular person has to have all the credit.

Sharing praise helps young engineers get past that tough time at the very beginning of their career when they may be assigned jobs that they don't find particularly interesting. "This is a very important point for young engineers to remember," an industry manager told us. "You are the ones who start out at the bottom of the ladder and who may get the so-called 'drudgework' that no one else wants. You have certain steps that you have to go through in the learning process, and drudgework is one of them. When you look back on it, it will be so much more meaningful than it seems now, when you are looking forward and seeing nothing but this boring work ahead of you. Keep in mind that this work is a test of sorts for you. It is a character builder. Now is the time to remember that you were hired to satisfy the customer, and satisfy the customer with enthusiasm and confidence. If you get your job done this way, then you are going to succeed."

One engineer said that he fought the drudgework blues this way:

"I feel that everything I do is meaningful. I recognize that there are times that I have to do work that I don't like to do and I'd rather not do. But I'm also enough of a team player that if I say my work isn't meaningful, and the company says, 'Yes it is, for these reasons . . . ,' then I will accept that and go ahead and do the work realizing that it is meaningful from the customer's perspective. It may not be meaningful from my perspective while I'm doing it, but my job is to satisfy my customer, and I take the attitude that if my customer wants it (and my 'customer' here can be the management, my subordinate, or a peer), and if I can't talk them out of it, and they're paying me to do it, then it must be a meaningful task."

One management concern that constantly stirs debate deals with the best way to assign a project to a worker. Is it best to give someone a job and include detailed instructions on how he or she should do it? Or is it best to just assign the job and let each worker figure out their own way to get it done the way that works best for them?

"There are shades of gray to that question," the vice president of an international construction firm told us. "Sometimes, if you kick a guy off a diving board and tell him, `Go to it,' he's going to flounder for six months. You can short-circuit that a bit by giving clear direction. On the other hand, if you tell him everything to do right down to the last detail, then what's the sense of having a skilled person on the job? There's no doubt that you have to help him get going, but you're also going to depend on him to develop something new."

Management vs. Leadership

The differences between "Leadership Qualities" and "Management Ability" are surprisingly complex. In fact, we found that you don't have to be a good leader to be a good manager, and you don't have to be a good manager to be a good leader. Each is a skill that is developed in its own way, and each is applied differently.

You can be an excellent manager, with the ability to plan, organize, staff, and execute, without having particularly outstanding leadership skills. You may possess the technical skills for management without having the sensitivity and ability to motivate others that is necessary for good leadership.

You can also be a great leader without having all of the necessary management skills. That's the idea of charisma. Some of our greatest leaders are people who rely on their charisma. Some people are able to lead others while they are extremely inefficient themselves.

"There is a common misconception today that management is bad and leadership is good," one industry manager told us. "But people who feel that way don't really understand either management or leadership. Management is a necessary function of business. A manager improves by picking up different behaviors over a period of time. We expect, in our culture, for a manager or supervisor to be an assistant, a resource person, a teacher, a coach, and a person who makes barriers go away so that people can do the work that they need to do." Good managers, he believes, are the unsung heroes of a successful corporation — the ones who work creatively behind the scenes to keep things humming along.

"A manager also has the responsibility to see to it that people are qualified to do a particular job," he added, "and that they are empowered to go ahead and do it." He said that modern managers are expected to follow what is known as the Four-Step Management Cycle. These steps are: Planning, Organizing, Staffing, and Executing. Skipping a step, or failing to give any step its proper amount of attention, can lead to the failure of a project.

In the first chapter, we discussed the concept of dual career ladders. We said that: somewhere in your career, probably around the fifth year or so, you will have to choose between a management path and a strictly technical path. But if you find yourself on the technical path, don't assume that you don't need management skills. Technical people who perform well often see their responsibilities grow beyond what they expected. One day they may be solving complex technical problems, and the next day they may be directing people to carry out the very solution they proposed. Don't be surprised if someday, before you even know what hit you, you suddenly become a manager. You need to be prepared for that instance.

The whole point is to glean the best performance you can out of each person. The trick is to be prepared to manage when the time comes. But if you really don't want to be a manager, don't follow the path any further than you have to. Our experts tell us that it's harder to switch back to the technical path from the management path than vice versa. Technology moves fast, so fast that if you're away from it for awhile, you can fall behind. You can't go back to being a technical person if you're away too long, but if you have good people skills, you can probably find a place somewhere along the management track.

Mentoring

For advancement in technical or management career tracks, mentor programs are very important. A great many successful engineers today came from companies that had mentor programs. The relationship between mentor and "student" is a symbiotic one. It's two people working together for mutual advancement.

"The older, experienced engineer uses his or her connections to improve the younger engineer's education, experience, and corporate contacts," an industry engineer told us. "In turn, the younger one does a lot of things for the older one to help achieve greater success."

He offered an anecdote from his own training to illustrate this point: "A professor who was in ROTC took me under his wing. I was commander of the cadet corps, and he was counseling me, allowing me to gain competence in dealing with groups and committees. When I did my job correctly, he looked good because he was in charge of the cadet group."

In other words, the more the student learned, the better the professor looked.

But it's tough to just go up and ask an experienced engineer to be your mentor (to say nothing of being a little embarrassing). Instead, it's usually best to select a person you have a great deal of respect for, someone you would like to emulate, and then just slowly establish a relationship. One of the best ways is to volunteer to help when the person needs help.

If there is no formal mentoring program in your company, one engineer suggested that you should just go up to an older engineer whose work you respect and start asking questions about the things you'd like to learn. Of course, you should do this on your own time. "People love to talk about themselves and their jobs," he said. "It feeds their own ego. They will spend any amount of time explaining what they do. That's all you have to do, just go out and pick the people you want to talk to."

Measures

1. Do you follow the advice offered by many management consultants that you, as a manager, should 1) make a decision on time when people ask for it or when you see the need for it; 2) provide the resources needed; 3) function in such a way as to make your subordinates look good? (If your people look good, they're usually happy.)

2. Does your work satisfy the customer, the boss, and the staff? Are you satisfied with your work?

3. How do your workers feel about their tasks? Do they feel good about them? Take a tip from Tom Sawyer; he was able to convince his friends that simply painting a fence was a great adventure!

4. How do you manage your time? (Time management is in the field of general management.) Are you done early, or do you rush at the last minute to get things done?

5. Do you have the ability to delegate? Do you do too much of the work yourself, without spreading it around to other workers on a project? Can you judge how much and what type of work to give to others?

6. When you dole out work, do the people come back with exactly what you expected? How clear did you make your initial requests? Are you improving in this area?

7. Do employees try to get to your team?

8. Do you have a good mentor? Are you considering becoming a mentor for a junior engineer?

7 Teamwork

Definition: *To cooperate with others in reaching a common goal in a manner that is satisfying or at least acceptable to the group.*

Everyone wants something different out of life — of that there is little doubt. We aren't all supposed to want the same thing. That's why roads are built for two-way traffic. Someone's always arriving as someone else is leaving. That's also why ice cream comes in a zillion different flavors.

The "do your own thing" credo has been with us since the 1960s, and in many ways, it has made the U.S. a richer society to live in. Today times have changed, and many companies have created teams to accomplish work. Some companies use engineers along with other professionals to work on project teams. As a young engineer, it is likely that you will be expected to serve as a member of a team.

The team concept has become more important, and more complex, with improving technology and society's increasingly global perspective. Today our teams represent more and more points of view. Road building is a good example of this. The advent of the U.S. interstate system affected populations, economics, and environments far beyond those traditionally touched by road construction. Interstate construction, and today rebuilding this system, has far-reaching consequences that will continue to impact future generations.

Back when construction of super highways first started, the attitude was "Get out of the way." Nowadays, parties affected by new road construction have to work together and reconcile differences through group consensus. An engineer must participate in these decisions with proficiency. The process is the same, whether the subject is roads, buildings, spacecraft, computers, or anything else.

"In my opinion," one firm's vice president told us, "engineering involves more teamwork than any other profession — lawyers, doctors, everything. A large civil engineering project, for example, can easily involve 500 or more people. The space program has thousands. The work of any single individual can have a profound effect on all of the others."

"Make sure you understand the extreme value of working with people," another vice president told us. "Make sure you find a job where you're not sitting at a computer by yourself, or where you're out in the back doing bidding for a couple of years. Make sure you are involved with some jobs where you are responsible for getting the building built, brick by brick, or where you're seeing the machine put together bolt by bolt. Learning teamwork is very important."

The idea of teamwork is perhaps more important today than it was 10 years ago. No one works in a vacuum anymore. You have to interface with team members within the firm and with people on the outside, too. You have to talk with everyone from the suppliers to the client. Today, there are fewer people who work alone. You need to interact more. In the old days, you might have a guy in your firm who kept to himself in his own office. You could slide a paper under the door, and he would work on it and slide it back out. He didn't want any help, and you didn't need to give it to him. For better or worse, those days are pretty much over.

"But," one manager warns, "if the consensus becomes the end rather than the means, then you are in trouble. Teamwork is crucial, but don't think that means you have to seek total agreement on everything. If you do that, you give the power of veto to any one person. He may be wrong, or he may be voting for the wrong reasons. Likewise, you can't rule some-one out because they aren't a team player. That person may be the one who is right."

An industry manager cautioned against equating teamwork with consensus. "Teamwork doesn't preclude making command decisions," he said.

"Don't be afraid to make your point," another vice president warned, "even if what you say appears to be out of step with the team. It may be an important point, and if we don't hear it, we all lose something collectively."

It's unfortunate, but sometimes office politics plays a part in the success or failure of a team. One vice president had a particularly bad experience with a company with which he was once associated.. "I was a member of a corporate board of directors where the chairman of the board once said, `I don't ever want to hear any controversy around my board table.' Now, that puts me in a terrible position because if someone drops a new issue on the table, I'm torn between following his concept of teamwork and my obligation as an independent director of that company to raise questions. That isn't really what we mean when we say teamwork. When we attempt to sit on any dissension in the group, we set ourselves up for the worst. We may steamroller the person who has the best idea at the table."

It sounds like that chairman of the board had a somewhat distorted view of what teamwork really is. It isn't a team member's obligation to agree. Your expertise on engineering issues has a certain value to your company. That's why they hired you in the first place. Likewise, the president of a large construction firm told us, *"I took hits* in my career under the heading of 'tact.' There were times when I didn't show the greatest tact when approaching a group situation. But those were times when I felt I had an intellectually honest presentation to make, so I made it. But that's always a judgment call. I just want to be careful that in enumerating key factors of success, we don't, as a group, put too much weight behind conformity." You can disagree without being disagreeable."

A lot of responsibility rests on the team manager's shoulders. When you're a new engineer, look to your team manager to set the pace. And at any time, when you're a team member, don't be afraid to step forward with suggestions when you see the group straying off its appointed course. When you're older, and maybe managing your first team, remember the importance of maintaining a balance, and be willing to listen to the young engineer who has a suggestion.

The optimists among you may think that a good team can head off problems before they occur, especially when the group has a common goal. But that's not always the way the world works. In an engineering sense, there is almost always a common goal — to get the job done. But in a larger, public sense, a team may be made up of environmentalists, business people, and civic leaders, and they may not all have the same goal. You can run into real problems. If everyone on the team doesn't have a common goal, anyone on the team can be a spoiler. The politician who has bet his or her career on having a public project located in a certain town may not want to hear from an engineer who says the water, soil, and other factors would make another town a better bet for the project. A manager who is determined to bring a company project in under a certain cost may not want to hear about your suggested engineering changes.

The Japanese are often held up as great team builders. Their teams seem willing to sacrifice a great deal for the common good, which usually means high-quality cars and electronic equipment. But some managers we talked to see problems ahead for the Japanese. "I think the Japanese are seriously handicapped because their culture is not diversified," said an engineer who works in her company's personnel division. "Diversity gives you different ways of looking at things, and in today's world, we need all possible types of input that we can get. We should study and learn what we have to from the Japanese. But we also have to retain what we need to retain from our own very successful culture.

"Along that same line," she continued, "there was a book written by Alice G. Sargent called *The Androgynous Manager* that said the best managers will have the characteristics of both male and female. They will have the hard, analytical male mind, and the softer, compassionate sense that a female brings to the table. Likewise, we can apply this same concept to the argument that American management needs to be more like Japanese management. We need to combine American diversity and innovation with Japanese organization and ambition."

The bottom line for the teamwork factor is this: People need to listen to one another and learn from one another. You synthesize the best ideas out of the pool that comes from the team, and you put the other ideas on hold. If you leave it up to one person to make all the decisions, they may not be the right decisions. Shared decision-making is what makes teams work. As an engineer, your voice is an important one in any team, but don't feel that you are the ultimate authority. There may also be political and other factors involved in which you are not well-versed. Try to understand all of the angles, act accordingly, and accept the group decision, unless you think it goes against the public safety and welfare.

Measures

1. If project teams were selected by peer selection, would you be selected? Which co-workers would you want to be on your team? Why? Can you learn anything from the people you would have chosen?

2. Do you enjoy working with others, or do you prefer to work alone?

8 Integrity

Definition: Fidelity to worthy principles.

Perhaps the most useful fable our grade school teachers ever told us was the story about George Washington admitting to his father that he chopped down a prized cherry tree. Real historians (the ones who aren't trying to teach valuable lessons to children) tell us that the famous cherry tree event never actually occurred. But for generations of American children, the George Washington story was an early introduction to the value of integrity. Society values integrity. Society values men and women who display integrity in their daily actions.

But in recent years, our traditional sense of integrity has been severely challenged. "There has been an erosion of respect for the principles of integrity," said an executive vice president of a personal products company. "There are a lot of young people today who think junk bond dealers and people who turn huge profits out of nothing are pretty swift and cool. We need to change that attitude. You need to be straight with people in everything you do. In fact, there's even nothing wrong with going in to your boss and saying, `I don't know what to do on this one. Can you help me?' That's the way you start building respect."

An industry engineer echoed those sentiments. "American society has shifted slightly in its values over the years," she said, "but deep inside the individuals, there are still some things they value as persons. They value honesty. They value trustworthiness. Of course, the easy way out when there's a problem is to blame society, or the company, or the other guy."

"Integrity," a company vice president told us, "is critical for professional success, and it is the only basis for enduring relationships. You don't do repeat business with a guy who lies to you."

Another vice president agreed. "If you don't have integrity," he said, "first, others won't follow you; second, you won't get any respect from clients; third, you won't be an effective communicator; and fourth, you will ultimately compromise yourself."

"I think integrity is the most important of all of the factors of success," an industry engineer said. "An engineer is in a fiduciary position. The community trusts his judgment. An engineer has to balance the public interest with the company's and the client's interests. In the final analysis, what is being designed must work, and it must be what is needed, not just technically, but socially, too. That's why integrity is the key. You're not just in an advisory position with your client. You were hired to make all aspects of a project work.

"You can't always agree with your client because he or she doesn't always know what's best. If you always agree, then you're nothing more than a hired hand. If you're the type who always agrees with the client, you may very well move up to the middle manager position. But don't expect to move beyond that. You just won't become a leader in your field with that kind of attitude."

Don't be a yes man or woman!

But integrity is a two-way street. You should demand it

from yourself and from your company. You want to place yourself in a professional environment that encourages integrity, not one that ignores it. Look for a place that incubates and nourishes this attitude. If you're in an environment that doesn't support integrity, get out of there. In the long run, staying there will hurt you. One engineer we talked with was proud to say he quit a six-figure job because his boss lied to him, and he felt he was being used. After all, he figured, he had been straight with the boss. The boss should give him the same respect. Integrity has to be a two-way street for there to be a healthy relationship.

Integrity doesn't just apply to your dealings with your boss. You need to honor your commitments with everyone. If you promise a colleague you'll run a computer program for him, do it, and when you said you would. Keep your word. Treat everyone with respect.

"The manner in which you conduct your relationships with other persons affects their perception of your integrity," a corporate engineer said. "You need to be honest with them, and this by no means is meant to imply that you always agree with them. Let's say you need to change your position in supporting your boss. Don't be afraid to change. Explain to him or her why you are doing it. Be up-front about it — this is very important. And don't just shift your support without telling your boss and letting him find out about it later. You can't be secretive. Be honest with all of your dealings. People will begin to trust you."

Along this same line, you must be flexible but consistent based on rational thinking. Otherwise, you run the danger of being labeled "unsupportive" or a "waffler." To a degree, integrity is trust. It's the things that you say that other people can rely upon. Integrity often means being willing to take the blame for what you did, or what you failed to do. "If you find that you're off track, it's very much like a child who has stepped out of line," said one vice president. "First, you need to apologize; second, you need to seek guidance if you're not sure what you did wrong; and third, you need to reestablish faith. At this point, your integrity becomes very important. You need to show that you will keep your promises.

"At this point, some people instead think it best to move on, to quit the company where they have established a bad reputation, and start over. Sometimes that works. But if the problem is a character flaw within them, it will always catch up to them again. They need to correct that flaw. This means working to improve their integrity, no matter how hard it seems."

Of course, as Rudyard Kipling would remind us, it's tough to keep your head when all about you are losing theirs. And it's tough to abstain from compromising your values when you see other people getting ahead by doing just that.

"I will never deny that a chiseler can appear to get ahead in the short term," a retired general told us, "and this is very discouraging to people of honor. But I do believe that if you poll the majority of very successful people, they will tell you that sooner or later, it catches up to you. The people who head to the funeral chapel with 'success' hung on their collar are the ones who made it in an honorable way."

Doing the "right thing" isn't always easy, but it's a lot easier than having to admit that you lied or cheated. Our research showed us that people are usually driven to do the right thing by one of three forces. These forces are:

A. Fear of punishment. You avoid the consequences of doing the wrong thing.

B. Appeal of praise. You seek approval from peers and superiors.

C. For the principle involved. You understand the values implied in a situation and respond in accord with the greater good.

Moving from point A up to point C as your "point of inspiration" for personal integrity reflects a maturation process. By far, C is the best reason to take any action, but A and B each have their place in helping young men and women develop a sense of integrity. When you're very young, you don't cheat on a test because you know you'll get punished if you're caught. As you get older, you value the praise you receive for doing well on the test without cheating. As you mature, you realize that if you cheat on the test, you are only cheating yourself. As a mature engineer, you should realize that C is the best point of inspiration there is.

"To an extent, integrity can be learned," an industry vice president said. "You learn from experience, and you can have both good and bad experiences to fuel that learning. You need to work with people who know what the proper role of an engineer in society is. There is no great value if the people you are learning from don't have any integrity themselves."

An engineering professor said she didn't want to brag, but felt that "Engineers have a balance of understanding that is very important to society. They can't just exist in a vacuum. That's why you often find them in non-engineering positions later in life — positions in the upper management of all sorts of companies, not just in engineering firms."

Many professions have established a "code of ethics" as an attempt to codify certain principles of the profession. Principles, that through experience, professionals have found to be worthy of their fidelity. Engineers have their own code, which says among other things, that engineers should:

1) Hold paramount the safety, health, and welfare, of the public in the performance of their professional duties.
2) Perform services only in the area of their competence.
3) Issue public statements only in an objective and truthful manner.
4) Act in professional matters for each employer or client as faithful agents or trustees.
5) Avoid deceptive acts in the solicitation of professional employment.

As part of the official Code of Ethics for engineers, there are also Rules of Practice and detailed Professional Obligations. These are points of conduct that all engineers should hold themselves to, especially if they want to move up the corporate ladder. The text of the National Society of Professional Engineers' Code of Ethics appears as an appendix of this book.

Measures

1. Do you keep your word? Do you ever have disappearing Tuesdays? (A "disappearing Tuesday" occurs when you say you will do something "by next Tuesday," knowing that the promise will be forgotten. Tuesday comes and goes, and you never complete your project.) Do you do what you promise, or does the promised date pass unnoticed?

2. Do others seek your advice on personal matters? Are you viewed as a person of high moral character?

3. Do you distort your message to avoid hurt feelings, trouble, confrontation, or responsibility?

4. Do you place the value of success before the value of truth?

5. Are rules important to you, or does the end result justify the means employed?

6. Do people say, "You can count on Sally to *do the right thing*"? Do they ever say, "You can't *count on Sally when* you really need her"?

7. Are you genuinely honest? Are you honest with your boss, with your subordinates, and with yourself? Are you honest with the public and your peers?

8. Do you betray confidences or play office politics?

9 Service

Definition: *Volunteer work for the benefit of others.*

What would you do if someone came up to you and said, "Look, buddy, I've got a deal for you. How would you like to gain a wealth of working experience in a short period of time? I can't pay you, but I've got a job that will only take you a couple of hours each week. It'll look great on your resume. It will give you hands-on experience in dealing with people, and it will let you move up the organizational ladder faster than any job you ever had. On top of it all, it will help the community and bring you in contact with some very influential people in your profession. What do you say?"

Chances are pretty good that you would say yes. That's why it's tough to understand why so many people fail to jump at the chance to join an active civic or professional organization. That's really the offer the person mentioned above was pitching. He was offering you a chance to do volunteer work for your community, your church, your political party, or even your local Police Athletic League. Or he might have been talking about the Rotary Club, the Lions Club, your school board, a professional society, or the local soup kitchen. He was offering you a chance to make a difference in your community and to enhance your career in the process.

Volunteer work is a no-risk opportunity to gain some of the skills you will need, such as management, communication, and group dynamics. You won't get fired for making a mistake in a volunteer job, and if you do well, you can move "up the ladder" more quickly than in a regular job. It's a good testing ground for your ideas.

"It's definitely an area that people need to do something about," said one vice president. "Look at the senior executives. Almost all have some sort of commitment to service. This commitment needs to start at the beginning of your career. Executives realize this. Your volunteer work actually brings something of value to your company. But, of course, it can't take up so much of your time that it hurts your work."

Wait a minute! Career enhancement, you say? That's not what public service is all about! Public service is for caring, giving, and helping others, you say? It's not something you're supposed to do to pump up your own ego. It's not meant to be a platform from which you launch a stellar engineering career! Public service is something you're supposed to do because you're a complete person.

You're absolutely right. In the most perfect of worlds, people should give of themselves without thought to how it will benefit them in the long run. Gifts of time and money for the community should be gifts from the heart. For this reason, community service is always a desirable trait, even if it doesn't give you a thing in return. Putting the welfare of the community above self-gain is one of the highest ethical goals you can set for yourself.

The reason we decided to mention self-gain right up front is for those people who don't want to actively participate in the community. What we're trying to do is enlighten the person who says, "I'm not going to a meeting on Thursday nights because that's the night for me to be with my boyfriend or girlfriend," or "I can't go help the committee on Saturday afternoon because that's my time to play golf."

People who genuinely care about the community are going to offer their help anyway, without any additional encouragement. What we would like to do is convince the person who always asks "What's in it for me?" that there is indeed something in it for him or her. Volunteering for the sake of career enhancement may not be the best reason for volunteering, but it's a far sight better than never offering to help your community at all.

Of course, if you do decide to join a service group, come in willing to work. Don't just join for the sake of joining, only to list it on your resume. Your presence will not be considered all that valuable.

One corporation president lamented, "Many kids come out of school today feeling that society owes them something, yet they don't feel the same obligation to society. There are too many people wanting to take and not give back. Well, you can't just take forever. Sooner or later, you've got to give something back."

There are plenty of people who are successful in their career who haven't given back to the community. But they tend to be the exception rather than the rule. And you don't find them held in particularly high regard in the community. One company president told us that community service is one trait that is almost universal among successful top executives. They are the ones whom you find coordinating the United Way Campaign or raising funds for community shelters. People who have a genuine concern for their community are the cream that tends to rise to the top of the corporate milk bottle.

Another company president told us bluntly, "Service earns community respect, and my organization wants people who are respected in the community."

"When you're first starting out, service involvement is not quite so important," a vice president said. "Your first priority is to see that you correctly do the job you were hired to do. Put your time and effort into that, first. But once you're established, it's nice to move into volunteer work as soon as possible. By the time you are a mid-level engineer, your service work will be considered very important."

"Service groups give you a bigger picture of how engineers, and those in other professions, really fit into the community," one executive told us. "By joining the long-range planning committee of a local symphony orchestra, I've met a whole lot of interesting and influential people whom I didn't know before. I feel I'm a better person for it. I'm not going to get promoted in my job because of this. But if I do get promoted, it will be because of what I learned through this and other volunteer jobs."

The bottom line is this: If you can do some good for your community, and in the process make business contacts and also improve the community's image of your company and yourself, then how can you possibly go wrong?

An executive of a telecommunications company told a sales-related story that he felt also applied to engineers. "We had two people," he said, "a man and a woman, who were being honored as top sales people in their regions for the sixth year in a row. When asked to say something to the crowd at the awards ceremony, both of these people thanked the people who had helped them during their lives and admonished everyone in the crowd to help other folks as much as possible. They said that they got to the top because they were willing to share the wealth and that it came back to them tenfold. I thought that was a wonderful attitude to have. They said that getting to the top includes teaching others along the way. In turn, each of the people you help or teach will have something to offer you."

The manager went on to say, "I hate to be critical of my own profession, but too many engineers just sit in their cubicles and don't develop their social skills. They need to get out more to help their co-workers and their community. They need to develop a sense of service. Everyone ends up better for it." One question that came up in our discussions is whether it is really "giving of yourself" if you give money but no time. Is it community participation to write a check but never show up in person to work? The group consensus was yes, people who do this are giving back to their community. But they are not viewed as personally committed to service. Money is better than nothing, but volunteering your time is the best.

And those who give only money are getting only satisfaction in return. They're not enhancing their management and communications skills by chairing committees and giving speeches, and they're not meeting the people who can broaden their horizons.

And what about the people who are very successful in their professional career who never bother with public service at all? "These people may seem very successful in their own mind," a vice president argued, "but not as much in the community's mind. That's why you really do need more than one yardstick to measure this thing we are calling success."

People exist in at least two worlds at once: the one they are paid to be in (work) and the one they enjoy in their off-hours (home life, sports, and other recreation). There is also a third world that many people exist in. This is the "other-directed" world of helping people and helping the community. To some, true professionalism means public respect based on the belief that the professional puts the welfare of the public before self-gain.

"I feel very strongly about being involved in the community," said an engineer, who with her husband runs a construction engineering firm with about 100 employees. "Everybody has their own `thing' that they can contribute. Engineers really have an obligation to support community efforts. We have very analytical minds. We can view issues with a minimum amount of emotional interference." She should know. She practices what she preaches. She and her husband have 13 children, 10 of whom are adopted. Many of those adopted kids are handicapped. While raising those children, she managed to carry on the duties of a corporate executive and earn a Ph.D. in systems engineering. Her family believes in sharing the burdens to make the home and the community a better place.

One final place to consider offering your service is to your profession. By joining and becoming active in an engineering society, you can help improve your profession. You can participate in local chapter community service programs. You can help with scholarship and guidance programs. You can assist in MATHCOUNTS, a nationwide mathematics competition for seventh and eighth graders. Perhaps lobbying your state legislature to strengthen engineering registration laws would appeal to you. There is a host of activities for you to participate in with your fellow engineers.

Measures

1. How many times do you say, "How can I help?" when community needs arise?

2. Do you belong to church, civic, or professional organizations? Are you an active member? Can you squeeze in some more participation?

3. Do you belong to a professional society? Are you an active participant in the society's projects? Do you give the society time or just money?

4. Be honest now, do you care enough about your community to volunteer your services even if it doesn't get you ahead in your job?

5. Have you joined a club such as Toastmasters to improve your public skills?

10 Ambition/Hard Work/Commitment

Definition: *Consistently seeking new challenges that go beyond those successfully completed.*

If you're going to be successful, you have to want to be successful. You have to be hungry. You have to be willing to give whatever it takes to achieve your goals. Unless you have a relative in the business, no one is going to walk up and hand you the presidency of a large company. You have to work for it. Commitment to hard work is a lifelong attitude that can make a lifelong difference in your career.

Hard work makes all things possible. Hard work is the grease that lubricates the elevator that will raise you to the top of your profession.

But that doesn't mean you have to beat your head against the wall every day. What good is success if you die of a heart attack at age 55, just when you should be enjoying the fruits of your labor?

"Don't go forth and seek a 60-hour week," a consulting firm principal told us. "But do go forth and avoid being constrained by the 40-hour week. Don't head out the door at 4:59 p.m. every day. Do what is necessary to get the job done. You don't have to be a workaholic. Don't feel guilty if you're not working. But if there is work to do, get it done."

Most successful engineers agree that their job takes more than 40 hours per week. And that means more than just putting in those hours. You don't sit at your desk and read the newspaper or play computer games. If you simply set an objective of being in the office lots of hours, you're not accomplishing a blasted thing. Ambition is having a desire to see that a job is done correctly, that it's completed on time, and that you "worked smart" while doing it.

The executive vice president of a long-distance telephone company whom we mentioned in previous chapters recalled how working smart propelled him to the top of his profession. "I changed jobs and started working for Southern Bell in 1962," he said, "and I was miserable at first. I was doing circuit design work, and after a couple of weeks, I said, 'My God, this is nothing but grunt work.' It just wasn't challenging at all. To get away from it, I used to go walking each day at lunchtime around downtown Atlanta. One day, after a few weeks on the job, I noticed this little narrow doorway with a sign that said, 'GE Timesharing Service.' I didn't know what timesharing was, but just out of curiosity, I walked into this tiny office and asked what it was all about.

"The woman behind the counter got out a few brochures and explained how I could rent time on a computer, and how I could learn a computer programming language called BASIC. I went back to the office and read the material, thinking that it might be fun to study just because I was bored at my job. But the more I read, the more excited I got.

"Then I remembered that we had an old model 35 teletypewriter in my building that could be hooked up to a computer system. I got approval to have a line installed, and within about two weeks I was never more excited in my life. I figured out how to fully mechanize my job, since I was doing simple cookbook engineering. I could just feed in the information I was given and use the computer to spit out the results much faster than I could do it on my own. I was doing my work much faster than 20 other engineers who were doing the exact same thing.

"The funny part is, when I showed my boss what I'd done, he threw my results in the garbage can and told me never to do that again. But other people heard about what I did, and I soon got promoted. In fact, I believe I was promoted time and time again because I would always focus on new ways to do things. I would work hard, and I tried to work smart."

The executive's basic premise was that, in general, an unfocused hard worker is not very productive. But a focused hard worker is. The focused worker understands effectiveness — doing the right things.

"It's not the hours you put in, it's what you put into the hours," he continued. "I realize this is an old saw, but it's still true. I see lots of people around me who work long hours, but they don't accomplish very much. They may say they're working hard, and they may feel the company is not recognizing them by promoting them. But the truth is, they aren't working very smart.

"I had a boss who told me once, 'What you have to do, my boy, is to pull a new one out of the hat every day. If you're just going to come into a job and maintain what's been done before without seeking creative new ways of doing things, then you're never going to make it.' Over the course of my career, I've found that to be very valuable advice."

That's the difference between simple hard work and ambition. If hard work means making sure a job is done right, then ambition means doing much more than you need to just to get by. It means going above and beyond the call of duty. It even means volunteering for new assignments, or suggesting projects to your boss.

Just as important is *the way* you package your ideas.

"I feel that creativity is almost a replacement for hard

work," one senior engineer told us. "Every time I start a new job, I look for the new slant that hasn't been done before, just to show my creativity. Now, I don't want that to sound like a shortcut because it isn't. You have to work very hard to be creative. But it allows you to apply your energies in a more highly leveraged way. You end up getting much more accomplished in the long run. It's better than just working hard and plodding along." In other words, it's working effectively and efficiently — doing the right things right.

One successful manager can trace his inspiration to a sign that used to hang on the wall of his fifth grade classroom. That sign said, "Many a man has failed in life because he had a wishbone instead of a backbone." He took that message to heart and accepted the fact that he could make his life into anything he wanted it to be. He was the one who would have to do the work. No one else was going to do it for him. And he was the one who would ultimately receive the reward for that work.

Ambitious people also have to have a certain intellectual curiosity. If a man or woman is going to be successful, he or she has to have some curiosity. You need to read, to ask questions, to discover.

But there's one more important point to keep in mind. Ambition is good, but aggression isn't. You have to keep your ambition under control.

"I was evaluating a colonel once," a retired general confided, "and I knew he was a very ambitious man. I told him that his ambition was admirable, but he shouldn't let it go further than it already had. He was doing fine, I told him, but push it harder, and ambition can be counterproductive."

The general recalled seeing a piece of paper under a table glass at a military personnel office that said, "Be on the job, not on the make." "That's pretty damn good advice," he said. "You can't let your ambition run amok."

In basic terms, ambition is the drive always to be seeking new accomplishments, motivated by forces such as intellectual curiosity, profit, recognition, etc. A truly ambitious person has to be in love with his or her job. If not, the ambition will not remain.

"I love my work. I get a high off of it," said a young engineer. "Most of the young people I know feel the same way," she added. "To be an engineer, you have to enjoy it because it can be extremely tedious if you don't. Most successful engineers enjoy the work they do."

Commitment can be considered an extension of ambition. In basic terms, hard work means just that — a willingness to work hard. Ambition is your motivation to work hard, and commitment gives you a goal toward which to direct your ambition.

"If I have an important job to assign," said one manager, "I'm probably going to assign it to the guy or gal who has a commitment to this company. I'm afraid that if I give it to the other guy, he might jump ship some day before the job is completed. I want people I can lean on and depend on."

But the U.S.A. has a problem these days. While there is no shortage of hard work and ambition, there does seem to be a shortage of commitment in some branches of industry, and it's not an easy situation to remedy.

"Part of the problem is that many companies have not treated their employees well," said a corporate executive vice president. "Engineers and others have given some companies the best years of their lives, and suddenly the company reorganizes, and the loyal people are out on the street. That lesson is not lost on the new people coming into that company. They say, 'Hey, I don't think I'll wrap my whole life up in this organization because look what you get for it.'

"There is much less loyalty to institutions these days, and much more loyalty to one's self. We can't pretend that people are still motivated by the old Horatio Alger theme of pulling yourself up by your bootstraps because they aren't. But in my company, we have found that there is still personal loyalty, and loyalty to a team. In other words, people still want to work hard to support their friends and teammates on a project, and to get their part of a project done correctly. That's a concept that our company can support, and it's working well. Being a functional member of a successful team is a way for an engineer to get ahead."

Engineers who come along today seem to have a need for what we call "natural teams." They tend to feel more loyal to that team than to the company. The quality concept in America has gained new strength these days. Everyone in the company can buy into quality. It's a good thing. The quality concept says that the customer comes first — either the external customer or the internal customer. By that we mean the end user, or the 'customer' down the line within the company who needs your work to complete his or her work on the final product.

Everybody has to have a customer. "Your commitment should be to that customer," the executive said. "I don't think you improve morale by working on morale, and I don't think you improve commitment by working on commitment. I think you work on them by getting all of the people in a team focused on a common goal. Typically, that common goal is service to a customer, not necessarily service to the company.

"You have to identify the customer and the customer's requirements before the team can do its job correctly."

Measures

1. Do you ask for a raise and then promise to perform? Or do you perform first and ask for a raise later? Go out of your way to be helpful. Prove yourself, and then you have the ammunition you need to get the raise you deserve.

2. Commitment is a long-term view. Are you loyal? Do you change friends a lot? Do you have friends you have known for years? How often do you change employers?

3. If you are ambitious, can you keep your ambition under control? Do you know the difference between constructive and destructive ambition?

11 Recipes for Success

Start off with solid technical academic credentials. This is especially important for women. That way, no one can argue with where you've been. When people want to get a handle on what you know and how you came to know it, a good education from a respected school helps to put everything in context.

Next, it's important to have a professional engineering license. Women especially should note this. It's a silent statement. You can frame it and hang it on the wall, and you don't have to say anything more. "When I got my license, some very technically oriented men that I was dealing with at the time said, 'I didn't know that you were that serious about your career,'" a woman executive confided. But the advice is just as sound for young male engineers, too.

Passing the rigorous Fundamentals of Engineering (FE) and Professional Engineer (PE) exams is an undeniable sign of achievement and initiative. It's best to take both exams as early as possible in your career. The FE should be taken while still in college normally during the senior year or immediately following graduation. You may not see an immediate need for a PE license especially if your employer doesn't require it. However, engineers who have taken the exams feel they were worth taking and have the comfort in knowing other jobs may come along that require a license.

Next are solid communication skills, especially in speaking and writing. More so speaking because we talk much more than we write. Practice your voice, tone, and inflection. Those can convey a lot more than you think. Never turn down an opportunity to make a presentation. This is also very important to being a good listener.

Also, work on your professional appearance. Look the part that you want to portray. There are books one can purchase on dressing well. You don't need to spend a fortune on an expensive wardrobe, but your appearance should be appropriate for the audience you are addressing. In one case you may want to wear a suit and tie and another sport shirt and slacks.

You should prepare yourself in your chosen field. Then you've got to understand the unique value that you bring to a company and use it to your advantage. After you get past the broad-based experience level, concentrate on your specialty area.

You need to know how to interface with people in the natural teaming environment. You also must have a notion of quality for the customer and be willing to serve the customer's needs.

Finally, you have to realize that you're never "there." Your engineering career is a journey. You need to continue improving your skills and never stop learning.

This book is about success in engineering. Success isn't a pot of gold that's over the horizon, always out of reach. It's something you can have right now, today and every day throughout your career. You can be a successful novice in the field, and you can someday be a successful senior executive. If we helped point you toward success (whatever your definition of it is), then we have achieved a measure of success ourselves.

Appendices

**National Society of
Professional Engineers®**

NSPE Code of Ethics for Engineers

Preamble

Engineering is an important and learned profession. As members of this profession, engineers are expected to exhibit the highest standards of honesty and integrity. Engineering has a direct and vital impact on the quality of life for all people. Accordingly, the services provided by engineers require honesty, impartiality, fairness and equity, and must be dedicated to the protection of the public health, safety, and welfare. Engineers must perform under a standard of professional behavior that requires adherence to the highest principles of ethical conduct.

I. Fundamental Canons

Engineers, in the fulfillment of their professional duties, shall:
1. Hold paramount the safety, health and welfare of the public.
2. Perform services only in areas of their competence.
3. Issue public statements only in an objective and truthful manner.
4. Act for each employer or client as faithful agents or trustees.
5. Avoid deceptive acts.
6. Conduct themselves honorably, responsibly, ethically, and lawfully so as to enhance the honor, reputation, and usefulness of the profession.

II. Rules of Practice

1. Engineers shall hold paramount the safety, health, and welfare of the public.
   a. If engineers' judgment is overruled under circumstances that endanger life or property, they shall notify their employer or client and such other authority as may be appropriate.
   b. Engineers shall approve only those engineering documents that are in conformity with applicable standards.
   c. Engineers shall not reveal facts, data or information without the prior consent of the client or employer except as authorized or required by law or this Code.
   d. Engineers shall not permit the use of their name or associate in business ventures with any person or firm that they believe are engaged in fraudulent or dishonest enterprise.

e. Engineers having knowledge of any alleged violation of this Code shall report thereon to appropriate professional bodies and, when relevant, also to public authorities, and cooperate with the proper authorities in furnishing such information or assistance as may be required.

2. Engineers shall perform services only in the areas of their competence.
   a. Engineers shall undertake assignments only when qualified by education or experience in the specific technical fields involved.
   b. Engineers shall not affix their signatures to any plans or documents dealing with subject matter in which they lack competence, nor to any plan or document not prepared under their direction and control.
   c. Engineers may accept assignments and assume responsibility for coordination of an entire project and sign and seal the engineering documents for the entire project, provided that each technical segment is signed and sealed only by the qualified engineers who prepared the segment.

3. Engineers shall issue public statements only in an objective and truthful manner.
   a. Engineers shall be objective and truthful in professional reports, statements, or testimony. They shall include all relevant and pertinent information in such reports, statements, or testimony, which should bear the date indicating when it was current.
   b. Engineers may express publicly technical opinions that are founded upon knowledge of the facts and competence in the subject matter.
   c. Engineers shall issue no statements, criticisms, or arguments on technical matters that are inspired or paid for by interested parties, unless they have prefaced their comments by explicitly identifying the interested parties on whose behalf they are speaking, and by revealing the existence of any interest the engineers may have in the matters.

4. Engineers shall act for each employer or client as faithful agents or trustees.
   a. Engineers shall disclose all known or potential conflicts of interest that could influence or appear to influence their judgment or the quality of their services.
   b. Engineers shall not accept compensation, financial or otherwise, from more than one party for services on the same project, or for services pertaining to the same project, unless the circumstances are fully disclosed and agreed to by all interested parties.
   c. Engineers shall not solicit or accept financial or other valuable consideration, directly or indirectly, from outside agents in connection with the work for which they are responsible.

   d. Engineers in public service as members, advisors, or employees of a governmental or quasi-governmental body or department shall not participate in decisions with respect to services solicited or provided by them or their organizations in private or public engineering practice.

   e. Engineers shall not solicit or accept a contract from a governmental body on which a principal or officer of their organization serves as a member.

5. Engineers shall avoid deceptive acts.

   a. Engineers shall not falsify their qualifications or permit misrepresentation of their or their associates' qualifications. They shall not misrepresent or exaggerate their responsibility in or for the subject matter of prior assignments. Brochures or other presentations incident to the solicitation of employment shall not misrepresent pertinent facts concerning employers, employees, associates, joint venturers, or past accomplishments.

   b. Engineers shall not offer, give, solicit or receive, either directly or indirectly, any contribution to influence the award of a contract by public authority, or which may be reasonably construed by the public as having the effect of intent to influencing the awarding of a contract. They shall not offer any gift or other valuable consideration in order to secure work. They shall not pay a commission, percentage, or brokerage fee in order to secure work, except to a bona fide employee or bona fide established commercial or marketing agencies retained by them.

III. Professional Obligations

1. Engineers shall be guided in all their relations by the highest standards of honesty and integrity.

a. Engineers shall acknowledge their errors and shall not distort or alter the facts.

b. Engineers shall advise their clients or employers when they believe a project will not be successful.

c. Engineers shall not accept outside employment to the detriment of their regular work or interest. Before accepting any outside engineering employment they will notify their employers.

d. Engineers shall not attempt to attract an engineer from another employer by false or misleading pretenses.

e. Engineers shall not promote their own interest at the expense of the dignity and integrity of the profession.

2. Engineers shall at all times strive to serve the public interest.
   a. Engineers shall seek opportunities to participate in civic affairs; career guidance for youths; and work for the advancement of the safety, health and well-being of their community.
   b. Engineers shall not complete, sign, or seal plans and/or specifications that are not in conformity with applicable engineering standards. If the client or employer insists on such unprofessional conduct, they shall notify the proper authorities and withdraw from further service on the project.
   c. Engineers shall endeavor to extend public knowledge and appreciation of engineering and its achievements.

3. Engineers shall avoid all conduct or practice that deceives the public.
   a. Engineers shall avoid the use of statements containing a material misrepresentation of fact or omitting a material fact.
   b. Consistent with the foregoing, Engineers may advertise for recruitment of personnel.
   c. Consistent with the foregoing, Engineers may prepare articles for the lay or technical press, but such articles shall not imply credit to the author for work performed by others.

4. Engineers shall not disclose, without consent, confidential information concerning the business affairs or technical processes of any present or former client or employer, or public body on which they serve.
   a. Engineers shall not, without the consent of all interested parties, promote or arrange for new employment or practice in connection with a specific project for which the Engineer has gained particular and specialized knowledge.
   b. Engineers shall not, without the consent of all interested parties, participate in or represent an adversary interest in connection with a specific project or proceeding in which the Engineer has gained particular specialized knowledge on behalf of a former client or employer.

5. Engineers shall not be influenced in their professional duties by conflicting interests.
   a. Engineers shall not accept financial or other considerations, including free engineering designs, from material or equipment suppliers for specifying their product.
   b. Engineers shall not accept commissions or allowances, directly or indirectly, from contractors or other parties dealing with clients or employers of the Engineer in connection with work for which the Engineer is responsible.

6. Engineers shall not attempt to obtain employment or advancement or professional engagements by untruthfully criticizing other engineers, or by other improper or questionable methods.

   a. Engineers shall not request, propose, or accept a commission on a contingent basis under circumstances in which their judgment may be compromised.

   b. Engineers in salaried positions shall accept part-time engineering work only to the extent consistent with policies of the employer and in accordance with ethical considerations.

   c. Engineers shall not, without consent, use equipment, supplies, laboratory, or office facilities of an employer to carry on outside private practice.

7. Engineers shall not attempt to injure, maliciously or falsely, directly or indirectly, the professional reputation, prospects, practice, or employment of other engineers. Engineers who believe others are guilty of unethical or illegal practice shall present such information to the proper authority for action.

   a. Engineers in private practice shall not review the work of another engineer for the same client, except with the knowledge of such engineer, or unless the connection of such engineer with the work has been terminated.

   b. Engineers in governmental, industrial, or educational employ are entitled to review and evaluate the work of other engineers when so required by their employment duties.

   c. Engineers in sales or industrial employ are entitled to make engineering comparisons of represented products with products of other suppliers.

8. Engineers shall accept personal responsibility for their professional activities, provided, however, that Engineers may seek indemnification for services arising out of their practice for other than gross negligence, where the Engineer's interests cannot otherwise be protected.

   a. Engineers shall conform with state registration laws in the practice of engineering.

   b. Engineers shall not use association with a nonengineer, a corporation, or partnership as a "cloak" for unethical acts.

9. Engineers shall give credit for engineering work to those to whom credit is due, and will recognize the proprietary interests of others.

   a. Engineers shall, whenever possible, name the person or persons who may be individually responsible for designs, inventions, writings, or other accomplishments.

b. Engineers using designs supplied by a client recognize that the designs remain the property of the client and may not be duplicated by the Engineer for others without express permission.
c. Engineers, before undertaking work for others in connection with which the Engineer may make improvements, plans, designs, inventions, or other records that may justify copyrights or patents, should enter into a positive agreement regarding ownership.
d. Engineers' designs, data, records, and notes referring exclusively to an employer's work are the employer's property. Employer should indemnify the Engineer for use of the information for any purpose other than the original purpose.

As Revised February 2001

"By order of the United States District Court for the District of Columbia, former Section 11(c) of the NSPE Code of Ethics prohibiting competitive bidding, and all policy statements, opinions, rulings or other guidelines interpreting its scope, have been rescinded as unlawfully interfering with the legal right of engineers, protected under the antitrust laws, to provide price information to prospective clients; accordingly, nothing contained in the NSPE Code of Ethics, policy statements, opinions, rulings or other guidelines prohibits the submission of price quotations or competitive bids for engineering services at any time or in any amount."

Statement by NSPE Executive Committee:
In order to correct misunderstandings which have been indicated in some instances since the issuance of the Supreme Court decision and the entry of the Final Judgment, it is noted that in its decision of April 25, 1978, the Supreme Court of the United States declared: "The Sherman Act does not require competitive bidding."

It is further noted that as made clear in the Supreme Court decision:
1. Engineers and firms may individually refuse to bid for engineering services.
2. Clients are not required to seek bids for engineering services.
3. Federal, state, and local laws governing procedures to procure engineering services are not affected, and remain in full force and effect.
4. State societies and local chapters are free to actively and aggressively seek legislation for professional selection and negotiation procedures by public agencies.
5. State registration board rules of professional conduct, including rules prohibiting competitive bidding for engineering services, are not affect-

ed and remain in full force and effect. State registration boards with authority to adopt rules of professional conduct may adopt rules governing procedures to obtain engineering services.

6. As noted by the Supreme Court, "nothing in the judgment prevents NSPE and its members from attempting to influence governmental action . . ."

NOTE: In regard to the question of application of the Code to corporations vis-à-vis real persons, business form or type should not negate nor influence conformance of individuals to the Code. The Code deals with professional services, which services must be performed by real persons. Real persons in turn establish and implement policies within business structures. The Code is clearly written to apply to the Engineer and items incumbent on members of NSPE to endeavor to live up to its provisions. This applies to all pertinent sections of the Code.

Becoming Registered As a Professional Engineer

Now that you've become an engineer, you should take the next step toward becoming a true professional — registration.

Every state, the District of Columbia, and the U.S. territories have laws regulating the practice of professions including law, medicine, and engineering. These laws protect the public health, safety, and welfare by insuring that those receiving licenses to practice have at least met certain requirements of competence, ability, experience, and character.

Registration laws vary from state to state and are exclusively under the control of the individual state legislatures. But generally, the registration laws for professional engineers require graduation from an accredited engineering curriculum, passing an FE exam, followed by approximately four years of responsible engineering experience, and finally the successful completion of a PE written exam. Some states may waive the written exam on the basis of education and experience, but the trend is toward an examination requirement. You should contact your state registration board to determine the steps necessary to meet registration requirements.

Why Registration?

Registration, first of all, is the mark of a professional. The registration process demands an extra measure of competence and dedication. While not all engineers find registration mandatory for their chosen career path, the PE initials after their name can provide many advantages.

Employers in all disciplines indicate that they find registered professional engineer employees to be more dedicated and have enhanced leadership and management skills. These employers look to registration in making promotion decisions in order to evaluate the advancement potential of employees. Registered engineers also achieve an enhanced status in the eyes of the public, which can equate the engineer with professionals registered in other fields.

Registration is an indicator of dedication to integrity, hard work, and creativity, and an assurance that the individual engineer has passed at least a minimum screen of competence. Of course, registration is just a starting point for professional growth and development, and participation in professional activities is part of the ongoing activities of a true professional.

Regardless of the career path you choose to take, there are a number of practical considerations concerning registration of which you should be aware:

- Registration for individuals who wish to pursue a career as a consulting engineer or a private practitioner is not something that is merely desirable. It is a legal requirement for those who are in responsible charge of work, be they principals or employees.
- Registration for engineers in government has become increasingly significant. Many federal, state, and municipal agencies require that certain governmental engineering positions, particularly those considered higher-level and responsible positions, only be filled by registered professional engineers.
- For those considering a career in education, many states require that those who teach engineering must be registered.
- With the growing complexity and diversity of modern construction processes and techniques, the engineer in construction must be readily able to communicate and exchange ideas and views with other engineers.

For those pursuing a career in industry, registration has recently taken on increased meaning with heightened public attention concerning product safety, environmental issues, and design defects. Employees have found it advantageous to identify to the courts and the public employees that they have met at least a minimum level of competence.

- Being licensed to practice engineering in your state or other states provides career opportunities that may occur in the future. Today many engineers will have several employers in their career.

Starting the Process

New engineering graduates needn't wait until they have four years of experience in order to start the registration process. Most state laws provide for a pre-registration certificate for those who don't yet have four years of engineering experience. These persons are generally known as "Engineering Interns" (although some states use other names). In New York it's "Intern Engineer" and in Florida it's "Engineer Intern." The requirements for an EI are usually graduation from an accredited engineering curriculum plus the suc-